Praise for
WHAT NEEDS TO BE SAID

"Alex Reegan's book provides invaluable guidance into how to live as your true self. He understands the human heart in a deep yet practical way. It's honest, authentic, and vulnerable, and in baring his soul he bridges the gap beautifully between his stories and me, as the reader. You will see yourself in this book. You will also see your way home to the real you."
Sonia Choquette, *New York Times* best-selling author of *Trust Your Vibes*

"What Needs to Be Said is an inspiring memoir and practical field guide to help you live a truly authentic life by daring, with all of your body, heart, and soul, to be even more of the real you!"
Robert Holden, author of *Higher Purpose* and *Shift Happens!*

"Alex is a burst of love and light and hope in the world. People are looking for new voices, new leaders, and new spiritual guides and Alex is one of them...."
Rob Bell, *New York Times* best-selling author of *Love Wins*

"Alex Reegan is an incredible advocate for change. He has developed an innate ability to truly connect with the people around him on a deep and spiritual level—at their core—ensuring that all who speak with him feel affirmed, heard, and seen. Alex's gift for connecting with people is lifesaving and his dedication to his community and beyond is truly venerable."
Perry Farhat, Esq., LGBTQ+ Healthcare Administrator, ROI-NJ.com 2022 Diversity and Inclusion Influencer, ROI-NJ.com 2022 Healthcare Influencer

"In this masterful book, Alex guides us through the experiences of a trans man in the modern world. We see his life through his eyes, experiencing the full breadth and depth of one person's evolution from self-understanding to deep authenticity. And through his journey, we ourselves are inspired to become our true self. He teaches us to live fearlessly, and with deep compassion for ourselves and for each other. He provides us a glimpse into the many gifts our society can receive from the struggles and genius of our spiritual trans brothers, sisters, and siblings. What Needs to Be Said *is the truth; in the truth there is power; only the truth will set us free.*"

José M. Román, J.D., D.Min., Vice President, Research Administration, Rutgers University

"Alex shares the heartbreaking reality of being a trans man growing up in a family where he is constantly condemned to hell. Along the arduous journey of finding Self, Love, and God, he gains deep wisdom that he shares generously with us all—and encourages each of us to start listening to what needs to be said. This is good trouble at its best."

Rev. Linda Bjork, author of *Inner Business: Training Your Mind for Leadership Success*

"This book is a fierce beacon of light and deep inspiration to return home to your truest nature, regardless of the roadblocks and challenges that you may face. It will help you to remember that YOU are the masterpiece, priceless and worthy just as you are. Alex vulnerably shares his incredible story, from growing up queer in a fundamentalist Christian background to his emergence from the metamorphic cocoon into the most authentic love-filled version of himself—now shining in his soul's true essence as a trans man."

Lainie Love Dalby, author and artist of the *Sacred (R)evolution*® Oracle and founder of the Ecstatic Embodied Leadership Academy

"Only through contraction can the spiral expand to fully flow into its own unique gift to the world. Rev Reegan's exquisite book takes the reader on a spiral journey through shame and hurt, into pride and healing, celebrating the divinity we are all born with, within. This courageous journey, shared with humor and deep wisdom helps reconcile the hallowed religious ways that no longer serve us with the bold joy that redefines post-patriarchal spiritual life."

Rabbi Amichai Lau-Lavie, Founding Spiritual Leader of Lab/Shul NYC

WHAT NEEDS TO BE SAID

WHAT

SPEAK YOUR TRUTH

NEEDS

RELEASE SHAME

TO BE

FIND ONENESS

SAID

ALEX REEGAN

HAY HOUSE

Carlsbad, California • New York City
London • Sydney • New Delhi

Published in the United Kingdom by:
Hay House UK Ltd, The Sixth Floor, Watson House,
54 Baker Street, London W1U 7BU
Tel: +44 (0)20 3927 7290; Fax: +44 (0)20 3927 7291
www.hayhouse.co.uk

Published in the United States of America by:
Hay House Inc., PO Box 5100, Carlsbad, CA 92018-5100
Tel: (1) 760 431 7695 or (800) 654 5126
Fax: (1) 760 431 6948 or (800) 650 5115; www.hayhouse.com

Published in Australia by:
Hay House Australia Pty Ltd, 18/36 Ralph St, Alexandria NSW 2015
Tel: (61) 2 9669 4299; Fax: (61) 2 9669 4144; www.hayhouse.com.au

Published in India by:
Hay House Publishers India, Muskaan Complex,
Plot No.3, B-2, Vasant Kunj, New Delhi 110 070
Tel: (91) 11 4176 1620; Fax: (91) 11 4176 1630; www.hayhouse.co.in

Text © Alex Reegan, 2023

The moral rights of the author have been asserted.

The information given in this book should not be treated as a substitute for
professional medical advice; always consult a medical practitioner. Any
use of information in this book is at the reader's discretion and risk. Neither
the author nor the publisher can be held responsible for any loss, claim or
damage arising out of the use, or misuse, of the suggestions made, the failure
to take medical advice or for any material on third-party websites.

A catalogue record for this book is available from the British Library.

Tradepaper ISBN: 978-1-4019-7117-5
E-book ISBN: 978-1-78817-872-3
Audiobook ISBN: 978-1-78817-869-3

10 9 8 7 6 5 4 3 2 1

Printed in the United States of America

For my younger self—your bravery and tenacious spirit got me here. Thank you.

CONTENTS

INTRODUCTION

"We're all just walking each other home."
—RAM DASS

When my guides gave me the push to write this book, they gave me a concept: that we are masterpieces, gems within rough stone. Our work is to chisel through the stone to the true self. And we do that by saying what needs to be said—as many times as it takes.

What needs to be said can be told in many ways, using many different kinds of ideas and language. In this book, I use the language that works for me. Yours may be different. All of it is good; all of it needs to be said.

> And what is it that needs to be said? At its core, it is this:
> Nothing can ever separate us from oneness. Nothing can
> exclude us from the true essence of Love, Source, the divine,
> All That Is—all of these words for what god truly is.

Let's unpack that word *god* for a minute. If you notice, I use a lowercase "g" in *god*. Although it is most common for that word to be capitalized, I've come to use the lowercase "g" as part of my process of reclaiming the word from spaces where it has been used to silence others and exclude people—spaces where *god* means one specific god for one specific group of people. As an interfaith minister, I was trained to look at god in many ways, using many names. Islam has 98 names in addition to *Allah*. Judaism has many too: *Yahweh*, *Elohim*, and *Adonai*, to name a few. Some Native American traditions refer to god as *the Great Spirit*. In more spiritual-but-not-religious circles, you might find names like *Divine*, *Oneness*, *Love*, *All That Is*, *Universe*, *Goddess*, and *Creator*.

In other words, our world is rich in language for the divine, and as you read, you might even come up with your own words or phrases that have special meaning to you. There are no rules here. I want you to use whatever you feel safest and most comfortable using. That way, as you are reading this book, you'll be able to spend more time absorbing the actual messages and less time getting tripped up on the language.

Having said that, I want to make a second point here. If the word *god* itself does trigger you—if it causes you to cringe or feel a little discomfort somewhere in your body, or if the energy of it feels off to you—notice that. Make a note in the margin of the book or write it in your phone as a reminder. (Similarly, if you feel uncomfortable seeing the word without an uppercase "G," make a note of that, too.) We will return to this later.

In my own reclamation work, the phrase I use most often is *the god within*—my name for the true nature of the divine that lives and breathes within and through us. For me, this language is useful in multiple ways. During much of my twenties and thirties, the idea of using the word *god* was very difficult for me. Even as I started seminary, I struggled to use the word. Over time, my healing work helped me realize something. I didn't want my understanding of certain concepts, like *god*, to be limited simply because of how other people might see or use them. Instead, I wanted to make these words my own. I also sometimes use language like *spirit guides* or *my guides*. For people who use language like that, it denotes connection with higher-energy beings—our spirit animals, our ancestors, guardian angels, or other beings who are on this journey with us, guiding us from the spirit realm. Perhaps you will relate to some of the language I've chosen. If so, I hope that sharing this helps you here on our journey together. After all, the road to everything we need is inside of us. We have access to all the wisdom of the universe—to all the beauty, truth, and love within. So, call that by whatever name you like!

Now that we've discussed language, let us return together to what needs to be said: Nothing can separate us from the god within. This truth holds great healing inside, if we could only live as though it were the case. The trouble is, our egos spend every waking moment of our lives trying to convince us otherwise. They tell us that we are separate, alone, and the world is against us; they tell us that we are less than, or—in the same breath—that we are better than, different from, or in worse pain than everyone else. And most of us spend huge swaths of our lives trying to heal this original separateness by frantically looking everywhere outside of us, while what we need was within us all along.

> Our work is to chip away at the things that no longer
> serve us, the beliefs that hold us back: the "I'm not good
> enough," the "I'm not lovable," the "I'm broken." The
> "No one has screwed up as bad as me" and the "No one
> hurts the way I do." The anger, heartache, self-doubt,
> and loathing that we cling to like security blankets.

> When we chip away at those things, brushing off the
> old paradigms and aspects of us that are inefficient,
> we make room—not for something new, but for
> something that's been within us the whole time.

Michelangelo once said of his famous *David* statue, "I saw the angel in the marble and carved until I set him free." We chip and carve to set free the true essence of ourselves. The true masterpiece. The work of art. The priceless treasure. The god within.

This has been my story. And as with all good stories, I want to share it. You see, I have learned that this work is something no one else can do for us—and sometimes that truth feels unbearably isolating. But I have also learned, paradoxically, that we can help one another in that work. Not by doing it for each other, but by sharing our stories.

In that shared storytelling, we gain resilience and strength for our own work. We find we can lift our feet and take one step more on the path of remembering our true oneness. And it's in that step we take—because someone has encouraged us or validated our experience—that suddenly we feel a little less alone.

For me, the journey to self-love has included stops along the way that I could not have imagined. Grace. Therapy. Weed. Giving up weed. Betrayal. Trauma. Spirituality. Shamanism. Rewriting my story. More grace. Some good friends along the way. Releasing old patterns and family dynamics of shame and self-loathing. Resurrecting the trueness of my divine nature that was within me the whole time.

And this will always be my work. In other words, my story is not over. It hasn't been pretty; that I can say honestly. My lows have gone beyond what I thought a low could be—and my highs, too, went beyond what I could have imagined. As I waded through depression, rage, and chronic illnesses lasting for decades, I sometimes wondered what it was that even made me get out of bed in the mornings. But something in me just kept moving forward: crawling, scratching, clawing my way forward, at times only by the skin of my teeth.

None of those obstacles—which tried to make me forget my own way, my own compass, my own light—ultimately succeeded. Somehow, they have made this journey all the sweeter, though to be fair, I'm sure I never would have said that while I was in the midst of one. On the contrary; during the worst blockages, the rockiest obstacles, I often wondered if I would make it out alive.

Of course, news flash: We won't! No one does. We all die. We all move on to someplace else. But while we are still here in flesh and skin and bones, we struggle and transform, finding our way back to the god that we have within—finding our way back to our own compass and guidance, our way back home to ourselves.

It is the most amazing journey.

For those of us who seem to have a million layers of difficult stone stacked on top of the masterpiece that we are, I think it's even more gratifying as we peck away at what encases us. As the stipulations and rules that others set out for us fall away, the shame and self-hatred that society has modeled for us falls away, too, and we start to see the true *us* that's in there. That *us* is where true rest, friendship, healing, connection, and peace happen.

> I have fought, scratched, and clawed my way through this life, and yet my fighting days are done. I've finally laid down my sword and my shield. And trust me when I say to you that fighting was just as hard of an addiction to release as any other addiction I've faced and released in this life. Fighting is what I've known. I'm good at it. But it's gotten me far enough. It helped me to survive; now it stops me from thriving.

Maybe you recognize that space. Maybe you're coming to that space, too. And it's easy to pull back and say, "But wait, there's so much stuff we still need to be fighting for!" I hear you. I have that same struggle in my own mind, the struggle of the *shoulds* and *musts*. But I've come to the realization that I can't determine what's right for others to keep doing; all I can know for myself is what's best for me. (Even that takes work to figure out some days!) I'm still in the process of overcoming this. In truth, it might take me my whole lifetime, or more than that. But through a myriad of techniques and modalities, I have certainly freed myself more and more, taking huge strides in so many realms.

So, what have I been chasing all these years—and what have I been running from? Ultimately, I found I was running from the fear that I was somehow broken and separate: a sinner, unlovable, unworthy, a disgrace. And what I was chasing was inside me all the time. I was chasing that true essence of the light within me, the god within me. It took me over 40 years of surviving all I've survived to see that this is what the god within wanted me to see all along. It was all already inside me. My coming home was a journey back to *me*, not a journey to becoming someone else.

Maybe yours is, too.

How to Use This Book

As you will soon discover, this book is part memoir, part guided meditation, and part how-to, like a friend walking beside you with compassion and encouragement as you do your own work. Each chapter tells part of my story: that of a trans man born into a fundamentalist and homophobic community, struggling through painful and harmful obstacles before finding his way to peace, healing, and his own integrated and true self.

At the end of each chapter, you will find a message beginning with the words "Dear Beloved..." that I received from the god within. I adapted this practice from one developed by the celebrated author Elizabeth Gilbert, who begins each morning by writing a letter from Love to herself containing exactly the compassionate and loving words she needs to hear. Since I learned of this practice, I use it occasionally to channel messages from my spirit guides, from the universe, from Love.

To get the most out of this book, you'll want to do your own writing exercises, too, which I'll help you with. You can use a journal, type into your phone or a computer, stick some loose pages into the book—whatever works for you. After each "Dear Beloved" letter that I share, I've given you a prompt to write your own. I hope you'll take advantage of this technique. Perhaps you will find that taking dictation from Love itself can be a powerful method of directing your stream of empathy and love—the stream that may flow most naturally toward others—to yourself. My hope is that both my letters and yours touch you, uplift you, help you shake free from things that are no longer serving you, and give you what you need to take just your next small step toward wholeness.

Finally, each of the book's three parts—The Origin, The Struggle, and The Emergence—closes out with a set of techniques, gathered under the heading "What Needs to Be Said About...," to use on your own journey. They include journaling, self-reflection, meditation, and other practices to enrich you and to heal and reclaim your connection to the god within.

Perhaps my story will resonate with you, or perhaps it will contain experiences that feel very foreign. Perhaps the "Dear Beloved" messages and the other exercises will touch you as they have touched me, or perhaps they will leave you scratching your head. I don't know. All I can do—all any of us can do—is share the story I have lived, and release the outcome.

I haven't always been able to do this. Sometimes I get pretty fixated on outcomes, so much so that I give up on the process. That nearly happened with this very book, in fact. Winter has always been a hard time for me. Whether it's the added darkness that compounds my fear and anxiety or something else, each year between October and March, life gets hard and nothing I try seems to work. During one long winter, I was ready to give up on this project as useless. But something prompted me just to go back and read what I had written, just to refresh my mind and see where I had left off.

I began reading, and as I read, I began to feel better. At times I said aloud, "Whoa, this is good. I wrote this?!" At other times, while reading one of the "Dear Beloved" messages, I felt warmth and love wash over me.

I finished reading, closed the lid of the computer, and realized that I had to finish this book—even if only for myself. I've lived and re-lived these stories so many times now, including in the dark, deep recesses of winter. And through all of it, this project—this reminder of never having been separated from the god within—brought me comfort and healing. If that isn't confirmation of being on the right path, I don't know what is.

> And that's the thing about divine direction. Sometimes the guidance feels subtle, like a little nudge confirming we are on track. Other times, it really feels as if the heavens have opened up and angels are singing our names. We have to be open to those variations in experience. All of it comes from love, and all of it is guiding us home.

So here I am, sharing the story of my journey, because my guides tell me that it's what needs to be said. I hope it might reach across time and space, and touch someone else's life, just as other people's wisdom has touched mine.

Now let's get right down to it and begin.

PART I
THE ORIGIN

CHAPTER ONE

WHERE IT ALL BEGAN

*"A journey of 1000 miles begins
with a single step."*
—LAO TZU

Looking back at where things all began for us may not be the easiest thing. Our pasts often hold great pains, losses, regrets, or unmet longings. Right now, I won't ask you to dive into your own experience, but I will ask you to come with me on a journey back to where it all began for me. Without that background—of my upbringing, my struggles, the trauma, the obstacles—the rest of my story, the healing I want to share with you, is not complete.

No matter where we come from, we emerge from our pasts with *something*. Burdens, lessons, traumas, memories—everything we call *the past*—each part presents us with an opportunity to grow, to reveal more of the amazing, love-filled beings that we already are at our core, and which we always have the choice to embody. As you read my history and reflect on your own, perhaps you will find that our stories, even if they are drastically different on the surface, have more in common than you expected.

●●●

Here are the basics you need to know: I got launched into fear real early and real deep, and I spent so much time feeling like I didn't belong.

I was born a day before my due date, and "one day early" was my pace from there on out. I hit the ground running. I always had a plan and something to get done. If a school project was due the following week, I would insist on an immediate trip to the store to get the supplies I would need. I had to do it *right now*. I never felt like I had the time to waste. I was always in a hurry to get somewhere; I just didn't know where.

The hurry, I think, came from almost dying of scarlet fever when I was one month old. I was in the hospital for some time. It was touch and go, and my folks weren't sure I would make it. Now, obviously, I don't remember this myself, but my family reminded me for years—heck, even decades—how sick I had been, and how I almost died. Something in those stories made me rush at my life for fear of running out of time, not getting to finish the things I started. That frenzy even launched me into spaces I wasn't ready for—fueled by fear.

Fear is addictive. Fear is seductive, even. Once it draws you in, whatever it is about that energy just pulls you deeper and deeper, like the gravity well of a black hole. Practically my first introduction to the world was through danger, and my fears only multiplied from there, especially through the religious beliefs my family eagerly imparted.

> **I was only a small child when I first learned to see myself as a sinner—someone who needs to be saved from who they are.**

I worried that maybe if I didn't ask Jesus into my heart correctly, or if I took one wrong step toward something unforgivable, I would burn in hell. By age six, I feared hell so much that I hated going to sleep. One night, riding home from my grandmother's house, my mother encouraged me to stretch out on the back seat and drift off with my head in her lap. (Hey, cut us a break; this was the '80s, before car seats—and even seat belts—were anything but a light suggestion.) But I couldn't. Every time I closed my eyes, the fear rushed in. *What if I did this all wrong and am going to be punished for eternity?*

Let's stay with that for a moment: someone so young feeling that paranoid. Really, what in the world could a six-year-old do to warrant being punished with hell for all eternity? Yet constant fear is the story of so many people who are raised in rigid families with very specific expectations and mores. For me, it was a fear of hell. For others, it's a fear of being hit, or being abandoned, or not having enough to eat—any number of fears too large and terrible for a child to bear. Over the years, whenever I have told a friend or therapist about this, I have always felt such sadness for that child version of myself. It almost brings me to tears, thinking of a child being that afraid.

For me, the fear never really subsided. It evolved,
morphing into other fears as I grew up. Even decades
later, when I made peace with my religious beliefs,
rethinking the existence of hell, the fear remained. What
I feared changed—the presence of fear never did.

Within the fear grew a deep seed of self-doubt. My mind was always racing, looking for what had already gone wrong, what could possibly go wrong, and how I might get something wrong (or certainly how someone else had!). Sometimes it felt as if the damn thing never shut off.

•••

As it turned out, when I was young, there *were* plenty of things to be afraid of—at least for a queer kid growing up in a family of ultra-conservative Christians.

Before I get too deep into the story, let me take a moment to explain some of the words that I'll use and what they mean to me— words like *queer* in the sentence above. Some of you are already familiar with these concepts, but I don't want any of you left behind because you don't know the lingo. Even more importantly, knowing what the words mean *to me* is in some ways more relevant than a "dictionary definition." If we asked a whole group of people, their answers would probably overlap with mine in some ways and differ in other ways, just like if we asked a group of people to define any other identity word or phrase, like *fundamentalist* or *spiritual but not religious*.

I like to think of it as part of the fun, and part of the aliveness and possibility of our world, that as we meet different people who identify as part of the LGBTQIA+ community, we encounter different relationships to and definitions of these words.

The truth is, I believe that our understanding of these ideas is going to continue to expand in the future, and that's part of why I'm not giving a list of definitions here.

And another important truth is that sometimes I find these words and labels helpful, and other times I feel flummoxed by them—like they are simply another way we fall for the ego's trap, the false belief that we are separate and not joined in oneness.

So, what do these concepts mean to me? For me, the word *queer*, which has been reclaimed by many of us LGBTQIA+ folks, is an umbrella term referring to anyone whose gender and/or sexuality don't fit neatly into a box, or perhaps isn't quite what society expected of us or primed us for. In a way, *queer* to me is about resisting the categorization, resisting binary paradigms like man/woman, male/female, or straight/gay. The truth is that humans' experiences of their own sexualities and genders are so much more beautifully diverse than that, and *queer* captures that for me.

As for *trans*, which is another important word in my story, I will start by sharing this quote from Rev. Dr. José Román about the concepts of sex and gender:

Sex is biological, and gender is psychological, even spiritual. Sex simply describes certain biological characteristics like genitalia and chromosomes. Gender is much more complex and speaks to how a person experiences and expresses their relationship to socially constructed forms called masculine and feminine. What our society does is take ideas about biology and turn it into personal destiny. Biology is not destiny. Human beings are not limited by biology, but only by our imagination and courage. The trans and non-binary communities are creating for all humanity a path beyond these social limitations.

"Human beings are not limited by biology, but only by our imagination." Let's sit with that for a moment. When we are born, our parents, the doctors or nurses, and the rest of our community make an observation about one visual sex characteristic (genitalia) and assign us a sex and a gender. It's a boy! It's a girl! *You will grow up to enjoy shoes with spiky heels! You will grow up to understand the rules of football!* And if the baby's genitalia don't fit one of the two things they expect to see, as is the case for many intersex people, the doctors quickly arrange for a surgery to be done as soon as possible, in infancy or toddlerhood. Case closed, right? Not really.

As Reverend Román notes above, genitalia aren't the only biological aspects of sex; chromosomes and hormones, which usually aren't looked into for a newborn, are parts of it too.

And as many other people have noted, you just can't say who a newborn will be when they grow up! Nor how they will interact with all the things our culture associates with gender.

As for the lingo: When people feel more or less aligned on the inside with what their parents and community and doctors told them to expect—or, to put it another way, when they feel that they at least fall within the expected range in terms of their gender—that's often called being *cisgender*. In contrast, the word *trans* is an umbrella term to describe any experiences outside of that.

Within the trans umbrella, people use lots of additional words to describe their own relationships to assigned sex and gender, like the word *nonbinary* that Reverend Román uses above, meaning not identifying as a man or as a woman, *genderfluid*, and many others. *Transgender* is one of the words I use for myself. At birth, my parents and doctors assigned me female due to one sexual characteristic they observed, and because of that, they expected my gender to develop a certain way. But that never matched what I felt inside my body or in my mind. I tried to make myself fit what they told me I was, but I could always tell: *That isn't me.*

Of course, in the late '70s and early '80s, *queer* and *transgender* weren't concepts that anyone in my circles was talking about. There were no LGBTQIA+ community centers in my area, no information I could find on the internet in the '90s, and when queer people were spoken of, it was in negative and demeaning ways. (Some kids today have greater access to better information, but by no means all. For an amazing dive into the depiction of transgender people in popular culture now, then, and earlier, I highly recommend the documentary *Disclosure* on Netflix.)

If I'd had that exposure as a kid, I might have made the connection and had an *Aha!* moment (or moments) then. But even without that specific knowledge, I knew in my heart that something about me was different from what those around me expected. Nearly a foot taller than everyone else during my whole childhood, I was a big, awkward "girl" who was drawn to boys' clothes and sports and hanging out with my brother and his friends. I rebelled against the dresses and earrings my mother incessantly fought to get me to wear. Many people have said, "You were just a tomboy." But *tomboy* didn't fit any more than *girl* fit. Before I had the language to describe it, a part of me deep down knew that they must all be mistaken.

So there I was, right in the middle of this evangelical family who really liked women to be teachers or stay-at-home moms, and men to be out in the world providing for the family, and who thought anything that wasn't Christianity was from the devil. So...a kid like me? I stuck out like a sore thumb.

•••

I am six, standing in the front yard with a bunch of the neighborhood boys we usually hang out with. I feel like I fit in. My brother suggests that we turn the hose on and run around the yard. We shove the hose down an empty gallon milk jug, and in seconds water is shooting out the top.

We tear our shirts off, tossing them out of the water's reach, and begin running gleefully through the sprinklers, finding cool on a hot summer's afternoon. I am free, full of life; I belong; here, playing with wild abandon, I am safe.

Suddenly I hear my name, yelled in anger. My mom stands fuming on the porch. "You put your shirt back on!" she shouts. "Girls can't go around without a shirt on." Our play, so spacious and free a moment before, stutters and grinds to a halt. I am baffled, embarrassed, then ashamed. Why has my mom yelled this? I look down at my naked chest and then at my brother and the other boys in the front yard. We all look the same.

Something must be wrong with my body, because she isn't telling them *to cover up*, rattles through my head. *Why am I different? Why aren't I allowed? Is my body ugly, or bad? Am I supposed to cover it to keep it hidden? What is the secret I don't know?*

●●●

That is my first memory of shame, and that began my descent into the world of body-shaming: feeling out of control in my body, as though it wasn't even mine.

Brené Brown describes shame so evocatively as the "intensely painful feeling or experience of believing that we are flawed and therefore unworthy of love and belonging—[that] something we've experienced, done, or failed to do makes us unworthy of connection." In that moment on the summer lawn, that's exactly what I began to feel.

> **There was no longer room for me to have that connection, to feel like I belonged—in my group of young friends, in my family, in my body.**

Most of you, I'm sure, know what body shame or pain feels like. We know what it is to internalize how Hollywood and magazines and the internet treat bodies: telling us how we should look, what we should weigh, what we should and shouldn't eat. Selling us millions of dollars' worth of cosmetics, plastic surgery, and Spanx to help us literally fit in to something. My experience in that moment (and many others like it, growing up) encompassed body shame, but it also went deeper. Not only did I inherit the ancestral shame that we thrust on to the female sex, including the hypersexualized way that we treat female bodies even before puberty, I also felt shoved out of space and time. Why was I being mistaken for a girl, when deep inside me I knew I was a boy like the other kids playing in the yard? In that instant, I began to fear I might never find a way to reconcile those confusing and very complex messages. And I knew that the rules I wanted to apply to me, the ones that applied to my brother and his friends, never would.

●●●

The first time my mother lets me select my own clothes for school picture day, I come out of the bedroom looking like I just stepped off the Miami Vice set, and I am bursting with pride. I am wearing a flowered button-up shirt, a magenta suit jacket, and a matching tie.

My mother takes one look at me and looks like she wants to sink into the ground. Every bit of her body language screams that she regrets letting me choose my own outfit.

●●●

Where did my preteen self even find those awesome clothes? Couldn't tell you. But that struggle was constant. "Honey, wear this dress and these earrings," my mother would say, as my fingers were twitching toward a ballcap and shorts and tennis shoes. I pushed to play baseball instead of softball; I wanted to do the things my brother was doing, not necessarily for the things themselves, but because I so ravenously wanted to be *me*—and because I so needed to get away from the version of me that everyone else seems to need.

Let's just say this struggle caused lots of ripples—tsunami waves, honestly—over the years.

●●●

I am 12 years old. My family has recently relocated from a small town to the big city. This week, my mother's good friend will be bringing her son over to our house for dinner. We are "warned" to take precautions when we meet him. "He has AIDS," my mother says. "He is very contagious. In fact, he's dying."

The night the two of them arrive, we awkwardly eat dinner together. My older brother scampers out the front door to play with his friends; later, I will wish more than anything that I had been allowed to go with him. My dad, totally uninformed and fearful about this scary "gay disease," leaves the table to wash the dishes with bleach. Before long, my mother dismisses me and sends me downstairs.

At this time, I have only a hazy understanding of what being gay means and how it might relate to my own feelings of difference. I don't know that transgender people even exist; if I did, it would seem even more dangerous. All I know for sure is that only good girls go to heaven after they die. Good girls are the ones who only like boys; they don't like other girls, and they certainly can't *be* boys! Any desires that diverge from that lead to spending eternity in hell. It's a simple "truth" that is never more real to me than on this fateful night.

As I follow my mother's instructions to go down to the basement, I cannot shake a strange, curious feeling—a sort of "knowing" that has come to me off and on for as long as I can remember, the feeling that my senses are perking up. (Later in life, I will understand this as a spiritual gift of seeing, of reading energy.) So instead of watching TV, I turn off the stairwell light and sit down on the bottom step to listen.

Our two guests and my mother are sitting alone in the living room. I hear my mom's tone change, a different energy emanating from her. It's an energy I somehow already knew was inside her, even though I've never heard it before. She is suddenly "preaching at," not talking to, this young man, in a tone that frightens me and reminds me of televangelists. I shrink into myself, there on the darkened bottom step.

"You must repent," my mother rails at him. "Repent of your sins!"

What on Earth are his sins? I wonder.

"Repent for being gay, and change your ways," she thunders. "Leave that lifestyle and never return, or you will assuredly burn in hell!"

This young man is barely out of his teen years. In his sickness, he weighs no more than 120 pounds, eyes sunken in, his sadness as profound as the deepest sea. He sits silent as he listens to my mother's barrage. She begins spouting horrific tales and terrifying "truths" of what will happen to him if he refuses to repent, declaring with total certainty that he is being punished by god for his transgressions.

Eventually, the room goes silent. My body is shaking, my ears straining to hear. Then I hear it: a broken, small sound. The young man, crying. He tries to speak, but his voice cracks. Finally, he chokes out phrases, bits of fear and pain, saying *I repent, I am so sorry, please god, will you ever forgive me?* He begs, he apologizes profusely, and he pleads for mercy, in terror of being abandoned by god when he needs god most.

There on the bottom basement step, my shaking redoubles. I feel sick, shocked, and, most powerfully, ashamed—ashamed of my mother. Though my 12-year-old self cannot say why, I know what she is doing is terrible, even horrific. Her words, spoken with such unquestioning authority, are causing unspeakable pain to a young man already on his last legs, body destroyed, heart broken. It is as though she is taking away the last bits of him, crushing his soul like a toddler stomping on bugs in the grass.

I can barely breathe, I am hurting so acutely for him. I cannot remember how or when I manage to stand up and seek refuge in my room.

It's not until later that the solitude just before sleep ushers in even more frightening emotions. I begin to realize the ramifications on my own life of that scene in the living room. *I am no different from that young man.* My mother's coldhearted, aggressive words ring in my ears. How much longer before I am the one on that couch, being blasted by her judgment? If that is how she condemns the son of her friend...how will she feel toward her own child?

A few weeks later, my mother tells me that the young man is dead. My heart twists inside me, imagining the pain he had to face, thinking of the intense distress my mother put him through in his final days. Knowing that that's what I will face if I reveal my true self: my family turning on me, and god damning me to hell.

•••

I enter my teen years, and my secrets and fears flourish. I date boys off and on, always putting on a good show because I suspect even then that my parents can tell I am actually interested in women. Unlike the parents of friends from other Christian homes, mine don't forbid me from dating—hoping, maybe, that dating the "right" gender will eventually rescue me from the sinful desires Satan is using to tempt me. Perhaps I hope the same thing. I date wildly, many more boys than I tell my parents about. One of them, an older boy from church and a friend of my brother's, comes around a lot, wanting to hang out or take me places. Sometimes we disappear into our basement to watch TV for an evening. My mother never comes downstairs, but dozens of times I wish she would—because Tom has a way of pushing beyond the limits of what I am willing to do, of treating my "No!" just like it's a "Yes." I keep this a secret, too.

But my deepest secret has a name: Allison. She and I are close friends, and no one knows how madly in love with her I am. In public, I am a "good girl," dating the gender I am supposed to date, but in secret I only want to be with *her*. She lights up my soul.

When she enters a room, I am filled with butterflies; I can't even eat in front of her. I know deep in my heart that if only I were allowed, I could love her forever.

I will never be allowed. I know this. My love for her is impossible: doomed, forbidden. We can never be together because it would mean sacrificing our whole lives: our families, our church, our eternal souls—all of it.

•••

Looking back on those years, I know I made many mistakes that I wish I could change. Yet when I think about that struggling self, I mostly just feel compassion. We all sacrifice ourselves—and sometimes even others—in selfishness or ignorance, just to survive and get through what we are facing. Maya Angelou says, "When you know better, you do better." Back then, I did not know better. Now that I do, I try to live accordingly. But in those years, I was trapped—assured, by all the people who mattered most, that my very self was bad, my natural desires dangerous and worthy of damnation. What if god never would tell me that it was okay to just be me: to love who I loved, to be exactly as I was without this attempt to masquerade around as some other person? In Jamie Lee Finch's book, called *You Are Your Own: A Reckoning with the Religious Trauma of Evangelical Christianity*, she says it perfectly: "I had been in a lengthy holding pattern, waiting upon external 'divine' influence to move me in one direction or another and to tell me what I could be free to enjoy and love."

Years after my adolescence, a therapist asked me to write down the things that I wanted. "Just make a list,"

he said. "Just buy a notebook and start making lists of things you want. It's time for you to go into your own desires and wants and discover that again."

But I was stumped—seriously stumped. I didn't know what to write, or even where to attempt to begin. My entire upbringing had taught me that it didn't matter what I wanted or desired.

In my upbringing, if I desired something, then that most likely meant it was sinful or bad. So instead of paying attention to what I desired, I hid from it, kept it secret—from others, and sometimes from myself. Pushing away my wants and desires was how I survived.

And when that has been your story for so long, how do you turn desire back on? How do you open those floodgates and allow desire in? When I was a teenager poised on the threshold of college, still not even admitting to myself what I already knew, I was years away from imagining those questions, much less seeking to answer them. I had a long journey still ahead.

Dear beloved, guilt-mangled soul, this is what I want to tell you...

Your ancestral line is filled with guilt and shame and self-punishment. This is something so many of your kind have passed down to one another over and over and over. You have been trapped in this cycle with them unknowingly, and not necessarily of your own doing. While you continued to cocreate the experience, it wasn't your desire to do so—it is what they taught you, how they showed you the path. And that path is one of pulling people back down when they get out, when they change and grow.

You have felt guilt and shame that you got out, that you've grown and expanded your consciousness. You think it would have been easier on the ones you left behind if you kept all these things to yourself—in fact, that's the exact problem. They wanted you to do that, to not share, to not push back, to not demonstrate the growth. But how does that serve anyone? It certainly doesn't serve you. Years of guilt of playing their game, almost entirely their way.

Would you like to play a new game now?

You've started it already; you've played levels and bits and pieces of it; it's just still foreign to you because they trained you so well to play their game. They expected you to believe that theirs was the only game there was. Yet you are about to come out of that supposed "one true game," out of the desert, and transition into a whole new experience on your journey here.

Are you ready?

We know that you are, but it's time you show that you are choosing it. While you didn't choose the path they laid out for you at the beginning, you chose it over and over again every day since they ingrained it in you. Today is the day to consciously choose this other way.

Let the new game begin.

Dear Beloved writing prompt

Take a few deep breaths and tune to the frequency of the god within you (or your spirit guides, Love itself, whatever word you use). The god within sees how shame has weighed you down and wants to help relieve you of this burden—and help you relieve yourself. Ask the god within: What do you have to tell me about shame? Where are the places where shame holds me back? What do you have to tell me about releasing it, setting it down?

Write down the answer, beginning with "Dear beloved...."

CHAPTER TWO

COMING OUT

"We spend our lives impersonating who we think people want us to be. And in the process of the impersonation, and the imposters, we either lose who we are or never discover who we really are, because we are busy impersonating who we think people want us to be."

—BISHOP CARLTON PEARSON

Coming into our own—owning our true self and nature—is never an overnight process. As humans, many of us are in a hurry to just *get there already*. We feel pressed, rushed, manipulated and controlled by time.

This is often true in our professional and social lives, but even more deeply, it is true in our inner lives, our journeys of personal growth and healing. We are so caught up in imagining a destination that will finally make us whole, whether it's that new job, a marriage, a baby, a new house, freedom from debt, or achieving perfect health. We are always anticipating arriving at that be-all, end-all moment for which we have searched so frantically. We hurry to get there...only to find ourselves not *arrived*, but still on the road.

My favorite image for this comes from traffic. If you have ever been on the road, watching a fellow driver speed by you in the passing lane only to end up sitting right next to you two minutes later at a traffic light, you'll know exactly what this human habit of ours looks like from the outside. (If you're like me and you've *been* that person, you'll know what it looks like from the inside, too.)

We rush to life destinations we think will complete us, and we do it as though we have no time to spare. Well, I am here to tell you a hard but freeing truth (spoiler alert!): that the destination you've got in your sights won't deliver what you're hoping it will. And that is good news.

There is nowhere else you need to be but here. There is no hurry. To truly get somewhere in our journey, we don't have to throttle forward in a panic. We just have to wait a few minutes for something to tell us, *Head this way now.*

•••

By now you probably won't be surprised to hear that I learned this the hard way.

Before I could begin the work of coming into my own, I first had to come *out*—out of the community that had only one clear path in mind for me. And leaving the path is never easy. When we set out on a journey like that, it is bound to ruffle feathers—our own, and everyone's around us.

At some point in our lives, we all receive a call, an invitation to enter a path that is unrecognizable to others—so different from their path that we appear as foreigners in a land we used to call home.

People react to us as if we are speaking another language. Where there was once unquestioned acceptance and understanding, suddenly there are tense silences, confused expressions, even anger and rejection. The loss of that easy belonging is what makes the journey so hard. As we release the labels and identities around ourselves that made us who we were, it forces others to release them also: to allow our identity to be adapted, to evolve, to shift, and ultimately to become something new. Let's just say, most folks won't be thrilled about having to do this. They'll find it threatening, scary, distressing. Yet, as Elizabeth Gilbert once said so beautifully, "Don't forget that every truth you tell is a kindness, even if it makes people uncomfortable; and every truth you don't tell is an unkindness, even if it makes people comfortable." In the end, our job is not necessarily to create ease for others, to make them comfortable with their feelings or their thoughts. That, in truth, is their own job. Our only job is to go on the journey our life has for us (and to manage our own feelings and thoughts when *other* people's journeys make us uncomfortable).

And my life's journey was about to come bursting into my little Christian bubble of a world. You see, "coming out"—to my parents, my family, my church—was not a simple, one-time event that I orchestrated. It was a series of events with few opportunities for agency or control. It started in my freshman year of college.

•••

Her name was Aviva. She lived down the hall from me, and she was amazing. To my horror, I found myself attracted to her. By the time we were a few weeks into the semester, we were seeing each other secretly. Now, at the time I was still uncomfortably identified as a woman, years away from stepping into my identity as a trans man. It was hard enough to admit that I was attracted to women, which would make me a lesbian. I kept our growing romance a complete secret, yet as I found myself more and more drawn to her, a new, astonishing idea began to take shape. Now that I was away from home for the first time, maybe I could try stepping off the path—just a little, just with one foot? Maybe I could have the freedom to make choices that were truer to myself? Maybe, who knows, I could even get to the point where I wouldn't hide my real self from my friends and classmates?

Alas, that point was further off than it seemed—because as it turned out, I was still carrying the "right" path inside me.

•••

I'm in my friend Samantha's room one night with a few other people who live on our floor. We're sprawled all over the dorm furniture, laughing, talking, swapping stories. Suddenly Samantha begins talking about her dad. He had been married to her mom for 25 years, she says, when he came home one day and said he realized he had been gay all along. "He said he couldn't put on the charade anymore," she says. "He couldn't be married to her. He had to leave."

"So, he just—left? Just like that?" asks another student, shocked. "What did you all do? What did your *mom* do?"

Samantha shrugs. "I think for Mom it was harder than for us kids. It really didn't feel like a big deal to me. It's not like our family was broken or anything. It was just changing. My dad was still my dad." She tells us how her parents managed to create a lasting relationship as best friends, and how they all spend holidays and other time together as a family still.

●●●

Now, one might think that this was an opportunity for me to see how people *can* live their lives as their true selves and still have family and friends—that they might not just automatically lose everything. One might think that in her casual acceptance of her father's identity, I might have been struck by the astounding truth that there was another way out there: something different from the scary, apocalyptic way my community regarded queerness. Something ordinary, with room enough in it for me to be who I was. One might think I sat in awed silence, absorbing this story, my heart filling with hope for my own future. One might think, "Ah, I bet this was a turning point in Alex's life."

Oh, it was. But...awed silence? Hope filling my heart? Not so much.

●●●

I turn toward Samantha, who is being so open and vulnerable. I sit up like someone has shot steel up my spine, and I pull out my Bible. I begin to tell Samantha...that her dad is going to burn in hell.

I spout off all the usual Bible verses about abominations and lusts of the flesh and men lying with men. I do a very thorough job of proclaiming his guilt and how terrible a sinner he is. My mom would be proud. It is, in fact, pretty much verbatim the same hellfire sermon I heard her deliver all those years ago to that poor, dying gay boy in our living room. It's been living inside me like a bomb waiting to go off, biding its time.

The whole time I am delivering this sermon, Samantha just sits there calmly. She doesn't seem to feel the need to defend her father, to attack me back or scream at me that I'm wrong. In the face of her calm presence, I eventually peter out. The night ends.

Things go back to normal. Samantha and I stay friends.

And I keep secretly sleeping with Aviva.

●●●

Can we all take a moment here to say, "Dude, what the fuck?"

To grasp the enormity of disassociation it took for me to have sex with Aviva in the morning, and in the evening insist (in front of Aviva, as it happens) that Samantha's dad was going to hell for the exact same thing?

And can we take another moment to appreciate the symbolism of the fact that I was in Samantha's dorm room, but the Bible I wielded during my tirade was mine, so...*I had brought that shit in on my own?*

Sometimes I think that maybe—just maybe—certain kinds of faith don't make for healthy, integrated, wholehearted people. Maybe.

And the time it takes to unlearn that level of dissociation is profound. Case in point: As I write this, I hear my ego-traumatized brain churn out a rationalization: "Well, if you were technically a man, because you are actually trans, then you weren't really gay, and her dad was totally committing an entirely different sin than you." (If I could insert that emoji face with the huge eyes and the mouth gaping open right here, I *would*.) Can you believe that? Even 24 years later, after having lived out as a lesbian for 15 years and out as a trans man for five—and after many years of working through my trauma and healing my childhood experiences—part of me still reacts from the PTSD of my evangelical upbringing as it tangles with the experience of being a queer person. It's still fucking with my mind.

Why do I share this? Because I believe strongly that sharing our stories has the power to liberate us and others. We beat ourselves up for not changing fast enough, for not already being where we want to be. But when it comes to change, healing, and unearthing the masterpieces that we are, slow and gradual is *normal*.

●●●

So much for my first "coming out" event—the appearance of that new thought, *Maybe I can do this differently*, followed immediately by the confrontation with my own split, dissociated self. The journey was unfolding, whether I wanted it to or not.

My body decided on the next "coming out" event for me. In my senior year of college, I became extremely sick. I couldn't keep from having stomach aches and diarrhea every day, and I constantly had intense tooth, jaw, and head pain. It was a nightmare. And I knew—somewhere deep in me, I just *knew*—that if I didn't come out, it was going to kill me.

•••

I leave my college apartment in the middle of the night and drive the hour and a half back to my folks' house. I sneak into my grandmother's old room and wait. When morning comes, it's time to approach them. I'm terrified, can barely summon the words. I finally blurt it out: "I'm not attracted to men." I watch as their faces shut down in anger and judgment, and I brace as though for impact.

My mom jumps into her response, clearly stressed and enraged by my statement. She goes on for some time, but honestly, I can't even process all of what she is saying. My father is completely silent during her tirade, and I begin to wonder, *Could he be more open to this? Could he at least calm my mother down?*

Finally, my father speaks. His voice is soft, his manner calmer and gentler than my mother's.

"There's a place," he says, "where they take care of that."

"A place?"

"They can cure you," he says.

Conversion therapy, I realize. I can still feel the fear in the belly of that 12-year-old, crouching on the basement step, hearing my mother pronounce hell upon that boy who had the nerve to be anything but straight. *They can't make me go*, I think wildly. *I am over 18; they have no legal control over me.*

"Dad," I say, my voice shaking, "I can't—I can't go to a place like that."

Instantly, his face hardens. "You *can't?*" he asks. "Or you *won't?*"

•••

I knew what was coming. The calls to repentance, the appeals to god and the Bible, the threats of damnation. But I wouldn't budge. I'd managed to get this much of my truth said: *I'm not attracted to men, and I'm not going to try to be.* As soon as my mother and father realized I was serious—I was *not* open to conversion therapy—the tone dropped down deep and dark. Doors slammed, voices rose, and not long after, my mother declared me dead to her. I had ruined her life, she said.

That day, I couldn't manage any more. I fled the house and holed up in my apartment, my whole spirit reeling.

Later that week, I talked to my brother on the phone and told him what had happened. "Look," he said, his voice filled with real concern. "I'm worried they'll cut you off. You've got another semester to go, and no way are you paying for that and your apartment on the tips you're making. Maybe take it back? Just for now—just until you're out of school and we can figure something out."

He was right. I knew he was right. I *hated* that he was right, but I feared he was, and that there was no option but to walk it back somehow. My authenticity mattered, but so did my survival. People who have had the privilege of belonging to the mainstream (e.g., if you are cisgender, straight, white, non-disabled, middle class, etc.) have quite a hard task in even trying to comprehend how much time we, as marginalized people, spend sacrificing ourselves, shrinking ourselves down to fit into society just to survive.

So, I called my parents up and told them I would "try again," meaning I would attempt to date boys. Some part of me knew that was completely impossible, but I heard the immediate relief in their voices as soon as I announced I was getting back on the approved path. My heart sank. *I'm going to have to try and sell it.* Anything to avoid conversion therapy, on the one hand—or the complete unknown of being disowned, on the other.

•••

The third and final "coming out" event happened not long after. Back at college, I was soon dating a woman, Anya (who would later become my wife). I was waist-deep in secrets again, careful not to tell anyone what was happening. That summer, I prepared to leave town after graduation and move near her. Soon—so soon—I would be out from under my family's microscope and freer to be me (maybe? I hoped). I decided that, as soon as I had moved, it would finally be time to come out to my family. At that point, I would send a letter telling my parents that Anya and I were together.

As the final coming-out moment approached, I began planning for the fallout. Around the Fourth of July, my family always had a family reunion, and this year would be no different. I drove down to the small mountain town I was born in, knowing in my heart this would likely be the last time I ever attended. I decided I needed to at least tell my younger cousins what was coming; after all, I knew—through both intuition and experience—that once I came out, there was a distinct possibility that their parents wouldn't let them be around me anymore. So, I wanted to make sure they knew I loved them dearly, and that if we were cut off from one another, neither they nor I had done anything wrong.

●●●

We go for a drive. I tell them that I'm gay. They're all teenagers—some younger, some older—and they seem to somewhat understand what I am saying. It's the '90s; queer issues aren't exactly commonly talked about—and certainly not in a positive light, not in our family nor in any other families I know. I tell my cousins that I love them no matter what happens in the coming months and years. Even if we get kept apart, I tell them, I will always be there for them once they are adults who can make up their own minds about associating with me. As I drive, a few of them pat me on the shoulder or hand, saying they love me; all is well in that moment.

●●●

It's one month later and the shit is hitting the fan.

It turns out that one of the older teenagers was acting strange, unintentionally revealing the fact that she knew something. Her mom pressured her into telling, and it all burst out: her cousin, a *lesbian,* dating a woman and about to move away with her to, as her mom puts it, "live in sin."

My cousin, scared, calls to tell me what happened and to warn me that her parents are going to tell mine.

Fuck. *Should I tell them? Get ahead of it? I can't—there are still a few weeks to go before I make it out of town, into my hopefully new life.* I am already finishing college like I'm making an emergency landing with no gear. Maybe they won't make good on their threat to tell my parents just yet. I only need things to hold for a little longer.

I make it through the last day of school, through the day of my move. My dad's birthday is a week away, so I determine that I will protect our fragile relationship until right after his day. Then I will send them the letter I've planned, telling them once and for all that I'm coming out...and then I will deal with the fallout.

His birthday comes. As I dial his number that morning, I know it's one of the last times we will talk before our relationship changes forever into something I can't yet imagine.

But when he answers the phone, he already sounds angry, clipped. All he says is, "Check your email."

●●●

The email I got from my parents that day admonished me for lying to them—and for a lot more I can no longer recall, because honestly, the trauma it dealt me caused me to block it out. In short, my cousins' parents had indeed outed me to my folks—the night before, as it turned out—and told them everything had been a lie, that I never intended to try and be "straight" again.

Things imploded in a way I could not even have imagined. I felt completely and totally betrayed by my relatives who outed me. I felt traumatized by my parents' response—an echo of the first one, but worse. *You've ruined our lives,* I kept hearing them say. *You're dead to us.*

It would be 20 more years before my family even began to mend this rift.

Nothing is ever quick or easy on our paths home to ourselves.

•••

In the midst of my family's fracturing, a second story of loss was taking place. As the devastation surrounding my coming out unfolded, I completely, totally, almost magnificently lost my faith. It wasn't an immediate severing, the way things went with my family. This loss was more gradual, taking place over the next several years of my mid-twenties. To this day, it is some of the deepest heartache I have ever suffered. Some on paths like mine leave the church of their own accord, but that wasn't what happened for me. I didn't leave; I was pushed out.

Word about me started making the rounds, and folks from my church community reacted almost in lockstep. I was the dreaded "g-word," and people called me to announce that they would no longer be my friend. This happened over and over. (The audacity of it still astounds me. I mean, who *does* that? If they had decided to stop being my friends, that was painful enough—they didn't need to call and tell me!)

My parents uprooted their lives and moved across the state, all for the purpose of somehow escaping their shame at people knowing about their gay child—the walking symbol of how they failed as parents. Or so my 20-year-old self intuited. I assumed shame was the reason for their move, given their prominence in a community that firmly believed queerness to be evil. My own father was a state representative for the governing church body of our denomination nationally; I had sat in the room while he voted against allowing gay people to be priests and against allowing gay people to get married in the church. I still vividly remember sitting, miserable, on my parents' back porch that evening as they and their friends celebrated their victory. At one point, one of them burst out, "Gay people should just get their own church, and leave us the hell alone!" The others enthusiastically agreed while I sat silent, afraid, and angry. Every fiber of my being wanted to scream at that person: "Oh, *really*? It's *your* church? You own it? You own *god*, do you?!" But I knew it was not safe to disagree—not then. So I sat there, quiet, long enough for my rage to pass unnoticed.

And so, my faith fractured along with my family. To understand the extent of the devastation this represented for me, I want to give you some perspective about the depth of my faith as a child. I loved Jesus, and I mean *loved*. At six, I jumped into my mother's car after Vacation Bible School and proclaimed "Mom, Jesus died for our sins to save us!" in a voice filled with infectious excitement. (Years later, my mother told me that was the best day of her life.) The passion I felt for Jesus was unforced, brimming over. Once, when I was eight or nine, we went to New York City on a family vacation. We were walking through Manhattan, and we came across one of those soapbox preachers: a man literally standing on top of a box or upturned crate, yelling about Jesus and salvation to thousands of passersby who mostly, I'm sure, were tuning him out. But I stopped. I looked up at him, eager to talk to him about Jesus. He stepped down off the box, and we spoke for a very long time. My family eventually had to pull me away, I was so immersed in the Jesus-talk. In high school, I mostly skipped the partying scene in favor of church and youth group, showing up multiple times a week, rarely missing an event. I yearned for connection and relationship with god, who was, ultimately, everything to me.

And so, when the fracturing happened with my family and church friends, I didn't just lose them—the people with whom I had shared my life, my ups and downs, my love of Jesus. That would have been catastrophic enough on its own. But when I lost them, I also lost god. That pain was the worst of all.

Perhaps for others it happens differently; they lose a church or family or a faith community but do not lose access to the divine in the process. For me, I lost god for two main reasons. One, it felt like my faith community and family *owned* god—like they had a copyright for god, and if they found me unworthy of belonging to god, I was no longer allowed access. Two, I could not reconcile god and my very being. Those first few years after coming out, I fought hard—in chat rooms, email exchanges, countless conversations— against people telling me I couldn't be gay and Christian. But it felt like a battle I could never win. I was trying to convince these other people, but I was also trying to convince myself. (In fact, maybe because I still struggled to grasp a truth outside of theirs, on some level I needed them to believe it in order to believe it myself.) My brain was ingrained with the deep belief that who I was—my being—was a sin. I was bad, inexcusable, and my life represented the worst kind of sin, because I knew it was a sin and went on doing it, rather than repenting.

So, while I fought this external battle against others, I was fighting a more devastating battle inside my head and heart. It was like I was screaming, "I'm still saved! God loves me!" out loud, while silently I was crying, traumatized by the fear that I might be spending eternity in hell. I imagined that all the "works" I had done through faith in god over the decades of my young life were for nothing, because my queerness trumped all that. It tipped the scales in a way that could not be balanced out again. I was done for. Toast. (Which is a funny coincidence, because toast is burned up, and that's what I was going to be....)

Out of self-preservation, then, I did the only thing that I could: I gave it all up. I walked away from everything I had known. I denounced Christianity. My faith. Jesus. I made this act a spectacle in my mind, a milestone; I felt that it had to be, that I had to sell it to myself. In order to survive, I had to convince myself that I was done, and that all that religious stuff was bullshit, made up to control people and keep them bound to the authority's rules and ways of being. If you didn't do things god's way—*their* way, in other words—you were out.

So...I walked away, and I didn't look back for quite some time.

•••

I'm driving down the road when I spot one of those iconic fish-shaped bumper stickers—the "Hey, look at me, I'm a Christian" symbol of the '90s, a slightly subtler cousin of "Honk if you love Jesus"—on a stranger's passing car. Suddenly, I am yelling, cussing, flipping the bird to a total stranger, completely enraged—and almost unable to recognize myself.

That rage begins making more regular appearances, and as it sets in, so does the void: a hole within me that feels simultaneously insurmountable and indescribably empty, as though an entire piece of me has died, and I am just a shell of myself still walking around in this world.

What now...?

• • •

The next several years were brutal. My partner and I ended up moving back to our home state, but all the relationships with our families were very strained. My body continued to fight back against this constant battle, with chronic illness that became worse and worse. I spent years on antidepressants, switching from one prescription to another with no improvement to speak of. My health declined. I struggled to go to work. But I just kept going. A few years passed, and we decided the best thing to do was to move away—even further this time, all the way to the East Coast. We had no friends out there, just my aunt, who lived a few hours' drive from our new place. She was the only family member who didn't seem at all troubled by my coming out. And that simple acceptance became a much-needed sanctuary from the pain of essentially losing the rest of them.

●●●

So...this stuff runs deep. Yours may look different from mine, but I promise you it runs just as deep for you as mine does for me. Wherever we come from, whatever we're carrying, we can each testify that it's been a long-ass journey—one we are still on, to be honest—and it hasn't been for the faint of heart. I came from evangelicalism, which taught me that I was a sinner. In theory, evangelicalism said that we were *all* sinners, but in actuality, it insinuated that some of us were worse sinners than others. I started out life believing I was one of those "others." Broken. An abomination. Hopeless. Likely not even worth saving.

That's quite a starting line, wouldn't you say?

It's no wonder, then, that I would feel an immense rush to get *somewhere else*, to a place of being fixed, to a place where that torment is firmly and decidedly in the rearview mirror. It's no wonder we all get so caught up believing that something "out there" will fix us—rescue us from ourselves—if we just hustle hard enough. And yet...that hustle is not our real path. Our real job is to *be here*, right here at this moment in our journey, and let the one next step reveal itself.

Back then, miserable and sick and far from home, I could never have pictured where I am today. I was deep in the struggle, and I couldn't see the horizon. My guides recently told me that I wasn't meant to go down a path that was just laid out, its grass neatly mown and trees and branches cleared so that I could fully see where I was going. No, instead I've had to trample my way through unmade paths. "You've done it over and over again," my still, small, guiding voice whispered to me. "Others saw tall grass, or trees so thick they felt they could never get through, and so they chose to stay on the easy path the world had set out for them. You saw that same path-less forest and got up, tied your shoes, grabbed whatever tools you could, and chopped, dredged, crawled, climbed, and clawed your way through."

All of us experience this, when we truly engage with our story. When the divine asked me to write a book and kept whispering, "You are the masterpiece in the marble," I marveled at how much and how long it has taken me to get to this place: to this understanding that I am a masterpiece, that I'm priceless, that I'm touched by and breathed into life by divinity itself. After all, my childhood, family, religion, and entire life up until recently conspired to teach me, "You're not a masterpiece. You're a piece of *something*, but it sure ain't a master."

Like we said at the beginning of the chapter, this isn't about magically becoming someone else—or somewhere else. This isn't about arriving. It's about speaking up with surety from the path that is yours, the path that you have walked in all the lifetimes you've reconnected and recollected— that you've chopped, dredged, crawled, climbed, and clawed your way through— and that you are still walking. *That's* where you can stand firmly and steadily in your own truth. It starts right here, at the ground beneath your feet.

Dear beloved, resentment-filled self, this is what I want to tell you...

We know, we know, you carry much pain and resentment toward many of the people in your past still. You wonder how they live with themselves so breezily after the ways in which they treated you. Even today, maybe they would still say it was in the name of love, or Christ, that they did what they did.

We are going to ask you to go inward and look at things on a deeper level. Are you ready? Here is your question:

What would it benefit you to let go of today?

You know the moment you hear that question that you won't like the answer. "No, I don't know how to let that go," or "Who would I be without that?" or "But then who will hold them accountable?" resounds in your head. Stay with us. Picture: What would it look like if right here, right now, you released the resentment and pain toward those who hurt you? What would that free up in your life? How much space would it open in your heart to be filled with new energy?

Now we want you to ask yourself one more question, a question that is simply the other side of the first.

What do you need to embrace? What needs freed-up space in your heart?

Can you hear the answer? There it is, ringing clear: What you need to embrace is yourself. Fully. As you are.

No surprise, then, that these two things are tied together, somewhere inside your heart. Your "people," people with whom you felt deep, true connection and abiding love, wounded you. They told you—or their actions told you—that you were not right and good as you were. That something was wrong with you. That you were flawed, broken, a disgrace, unsaveable. How could you help but believe them? How could you not then associate yourself with being less than, not good enough, and broken?

So this is the key to moving forward in your work. Lay down these burdens you have carried—which are *their* burdens, *their* stories, *their* actions toward you—and release the need to carry them forward any longer as your own. You don't need them anymore; you have carried them long enough—and it wasn't your responsibility to carry them in the first place, but we understand why you did.

By being willing to release their beliefs, their words, their choices—all of which weren't *really* about you, but just about them and their own fears—you are letting yourself off the hook. Forgiveness means setting yourself free from your past and the people in it. They have all long since faded from your experience and even, mostly, your memory. It's the scars that have remained. So, let's release this, all of it, together. Release the story, the lies, the excuses to be mean to and hard on yourself. It's time to move forward, embracing yourself in your wholeness, in your goodness, in your kindness, compassion, love, generosity, curiosity, excitement, joy, beauty, enthusiasm, and grace. You must be willing to step into the truth of yourself, because if you don't, it's not them who will lose—it's you.

Dear Beloved writing prompt

Let the god within answer these questions for you: What do you know it would benefit me to let go of today? What do I need to embrace?

Write down what the god within says to you, beginning with, "Dear beloved..."

What Needs to Be Said About the Origin

*"To forgive is to set a prisoner free and
discover that the prisoner was you."*
—Lewis B. Smedes

Look. What needs to be said sometimes isn't pretty or even easy to do. But we are going to start with some practices that you will hopefully find not only helpful but also reasonable, manageable.

Before we begin, I'd like to say that my hope for you within these practices is that you will be able to look back at some of your own origin stories and find a new way to observe your experiences of trauma—from family, from societal pressures, from all other pains—with new eyes, and with hopefulness in the potential of newfound freedom from these heartaches.

In these practices, we are going to play with one or two small things that are in our power to do, and then we are going to simply notice what happens. This is your opportunity to begin to find your truth and learn to speak it, when in the past it may have been clouded over by your upbringing, the trauma that happened to you, and simply the overall layers of weight that society buries us under.

> **The process will feel gradual at first, and the changes small. I encourage you to know and accept this, rather than looking for the huge and immediate changes we think we need. Sometimes, all we actually need is to feel just a little less shitty.**

When huge changes are the goal, it often hides the fact that there are a multitude of things we can do to help ourselves in a given moment. Usually these things are small. There are few, if any, things in this world that make huge, drastic shifts in us—from feeling like complete shit to sudden, total, unending bliss—and those few tend to be short-lived (and to come with a hefty price tag). Like spurts in a sprint, they are fast and get you somewhere quickly, but they aren't sustainable at that speed.

This groundwork, like any good journey, consists of small steps. And so, we are going to start small—together.

WHAT NEEDS TO BE SAID PRACTICE: IT IS TRUE THAT

For our first practice of Part One: The Origin, I would like to invite you into a technique that can help you get back in touch with your guidance system, enabling you to validate yourself in a new way. I was given this practice through a reading some years ago, and during particularly hard periods, I will do this for weeks or even months at a time to help reorient and ground myself.

In a journal, notebook, computer document or whatever works for you, write down: "It is true that...." Using this sentence prompt, finish the thought with only completely factual statements. For instance, right now I am wearing a blue shirt, so I could write, "It is true that I am wearing a blue shirt." Of course, you can write about deeper things, like emotions (for example, "It is true that I am wide awake and feeling calm," or "It is true that I can't sleep and I feel anxious"). But those are more complex, and when you have to focus in carefully on something that you can identify as true in the moment, they might suddenly feel too complicated. When you are trying this practice for the first time, it may be best to begin with something easy, like the color of your shirt.

When we have suffered things like religious trauma, our innate guidance system gets thrown wildly off track. For so many years, I was asked to put aside my own "knowing" and follow that of the church, of their god and their rules. One of the most important steps I took in reclaiming my own knowing was this practice of reconnection with my own guidance system, slowly figuring out just what I knew to be true for me.

Because this statement practice requires us to only write what we "know" to be true, it also helps us step outside of some of the stories that we have about the things that have happened in our lives. Using this practice, in conjunction with the next one we'll learn, will help you find your direction again. I say "again" because your soul-level self—your holy self, the god within—never lost this guidance. Only our ego self loses its way.

But don't worry—you haven't done it wrong. "Wrong" turns, getting off course, is all a part of the journey. In fact, I'm here to tell you that you can't get it wrong. Just as the navigation app on your phone simply reroutes you when you get off course, and then you're on your way again, this is simply a "rerouting"—and onward and upward you go.

Now write your list of "It is true that..." statements.

WHAT NEEDS TO BE SAID PRACTICE: REFRAMING THE WHYS

We get to decide the "why" behind the things that happen to us.

Now, this is something I've preached and taught about a lot, and it's always a space where people want me to slow down and explain more fully, because what I mean here seems counterintuitive. Normally, we think of the why as just a fact. We don't see it as something that we can decide or change. And very often, we either think that a) we know exactly why that person hurt us that way, and it's because they suck; or b) we know exactly why that person hurt us that way, and it's because we suck.

The only way to disarm the ego is to question that maybe we don't know the why—and ultimately, to admit that we definitely don't know the why. But the unknown, that "I don't know" space, tends to leave us feeling deeply uncomfortable. We would much rather feel certain. And so, our next option is to choose a different why—and we get to choose one that is less painful and blame-filled.

Let's take an example: my brother and me. We have struggled with our relationship since I came out as trans. He just can't seem to wrap his head around it or come to terms with it. And the last time we truly spoke, we got into a huge fight over it. Why? Now, the truth of the matter is, I don't technically know why he acted the way that he did. Heck, maybe he doesn't even understand why. (I think that happens to all of us frequently.) But here is the catch: My ego thinks it knows why he acted the way that he did. And the ego's "knowledge" often sounds something like this (see if any of these sound familiar from your own relationships):

- "My brother doesn't respect me."

- "My brother isn't on my side like he said he is."

- "My brother hates me."

Those are some "why stories" when the ego is sending its blame outward. Sometimes, though, it sends that blame inward, in a self-punishing fashion:

- "There's something wrong with me that makes people not accept me."

- "I'm bad, too awful to be loved."

- "Apparently I'm the sort of person who can never have my needs met."

Either way, blaming outward or inward, the ego's story is convincing. It feels so, so true. Here is the hill, and our ego is determined to die on it. If anyone argues with the ego, trying to get it to "think positive" or see things from some other point of view, the ego will simply fight back endlessly, and we will never get anywhere.

Now I'm going to change the "why" to something else, and I want you to see how these phrases feel in your body in comparison to the previous statements. Ready?

- "My brother is afraid."

- "My brother felt like he lost something he loved."

- "My brother is scared about 'doing it wrong.'"

- "My brother felt upset about something else entirely and, out of frustration, took it out on me."

I want you to look at the narrower statements from above and then compare their energy to these broader statements here. Do you notice the difference? Can you feel a softening in your shoulders, a warmth in your chest, or a faint sensation of peace, like a long-held breath being released? Notice that.

With this shift, we have moved out of separation into a space where empathy is possible. Because I can relate to being afraid. And I know what it feels like to think I've lost something I love. I know about the fear of doing it wrong, and I definitely have taken my frustration out on one person when I was upset about something else entirely. As my friend Andrea says, "I believe we can only tolerate the feelings in others that we have learned to tolerate in ourselves." When someone cannot tolerate or accept a part of me, sometimes that has nothing to do with me and everything to do with how they have not yet been able to tolerate or accept that part of themselves. Fear and loss aren't easy to tolerate—for my brother, or for me.

All of a sudden, my brother and I aren't that different. We aren't really separate. Even though our unity might not take shape in the physical world in conversation together, energetically, we've joined each other. We are connected in wholeness through the boundless love of the divine.

I want to point out that we can do the same thing with the self-punishing statements. We can change the perspective on them as well, to the broader whys below:

- "When people can't accept me, they must be going through something that I don't know about. Maybe they don't know how to accept themselves."

- "This person may not be able to love me, but I can love myself and find love elsewhere."

- "I am open to my needs being met in ways I cannot yet imagine."

In this shift to a new why, I've met myself with boundless love and empathy, letting self-doubt and the need to punish myself slip away.

See, this is the trick. We choose the why. In fact, we never knew the whys of our lives with certainty; we just felt certain. When we follow the narrow why, it is just as unverifiable as all the others. What is really going on is that we are deciding in our minds why people do the things that they do. And when we let the ego run with those stories of the why, we almost always end up suffering needlessly. After all, what did I accomplish by thinking that my brother hates me? Did it actually cause him to do something differently? Did it encourage him to change? No. Of course not. Did it help me feel better? Did it bring goodness to my life? Not so much! All it did is cause me to sit in the painful idea that I am not respected, or that I'm hated by my own sibling.

The idea that we decide on the why is scary for people. It forces us to realize the possibility that we have more control over how we feel in our daily lives than we might actually be comfortable with.

But there is so much power in this. It will change your life if you practice awareness around this and put it into action.

Here are a few more examples for you to consider:

- **Narrow WHY:** "That guy cut me off in traffic. He's such an asshole."

- **Broad WHY:** "What if that guy's wife is in labor?"

- **Narrow WHY:** "My coworker is so dismissing and takes all the credit."

- **Broad WHY:** "What if they are a perfectionist too and are afraid of failing?"

Now I want you to practice this with stories of your own. Use your journal, a computer document, or the like. In the future, you can continue to write down your whys or you can do them in your mind as you go about your day. But first, a word of caution: Start off with only situations that feel mildly frustrating to you, maybe even imaginary ones. Once you feel like you're getting the hang of this practice, you'll be able to move on to the events and people involved in deeper wounding in your life, but for now, the harder stuff would likely just feel unmanageable, which could discourage you from getting adept at the new practice. So, trust me when I recommend starting off easy and then going deeper. You've got this!

1. Imagine or describe the encounter.

2. Tell the narrow why.

3. Reframe the narrow why to the broad why.

4. Sit with the energetic feelings. Allow yourself the space to quietly sit with the emotions that come up with both the narrow and broad whys. Notice the differences.

PART II

THE
STRUGGLE

CHAPTER THREE

WHAT NOW?

*"If I'd seen the hills and valleys on the
road, I might've never had the courage
to pack my bags and go."*
—EMILY SCOTT ROBINSON

Life is cruel. Life is suffering. Life is pain.

We have all experienced life coming across this way at times. Our experience on Earth can seem so full of destruction, hate, pain, and violence, that it sometimes feels completely unbearable. We all struggle and cry out in agony and suffering. Our Earth is a very dense place energetically, and as such, the lessons here are going to be more intense, as we move from the chaos of forgetting who we are, into the flow and openness of once more recovering ourselves and our knowledge of the god within.

How could it be otherwise? The intensity of the struggle matches the intensity of the love waiting to receive us. After all, finding ways to love our neighbor—who screams and yells at the top of his lungs against the very things that matter most to us—is an extraordinary feat of love. Loving ourselves through the pain and shame that we think we caused ourselves is likewise an extreme feat of transformation and vibrational alignment back into our divine truth. (Also, as my friend Kezia once told me, "Loving ourselves is the biggest act of rebellion we can do when people try to bring us down.") We can understand these concepts on the intellectual plane, but it is an entirely new experience to actually live them.

And that usually comes through pain. More often than not, in this human experience, we need contrast to drive us forward. I know this is hard to hear; in the midst of pain, heartache, discomfort, dis-ease, and trauma, how can we see what is befalling us as part of the needed push to move us beyond ourselves?

Picture for a moment how transformation happens on Earth's physical plane. When a fire burns through a forest that needs renewing, the flames come not slow and small, but with an intensity and power that rivals anything in the human experience. When a blacksmith uses fire to mold and transform metals, she does not work with a low flame with minimal heat; she calls forth a heat profound enough to melt down some of the hardest, sturdiest substances on Earth. Transformation comes in this way for humans, too. It doesn't come in tiny, mild, calm experiences; it comes like a tsunami washing through a town, wiping out the very foundations of the beliefs and life you so painstakingly created. Everything that is created anew begins with an explosion of energy. That's how newness is born.

So take heart, dear beloveds: you are not doing it wrong. You are not alone in this, and you aren't simply being tortured for the sake of torture. There is deep, abiding transformation at hand.

●●●

The early 2000s found me just out of college, freshly outed against my will to my parents, and recently moved (escaped!) to the East Coast. Deep, abiding transformation was not on my mind; most days I felt as though I were barely getting through. Some part of me constantly felt like I was outrunning something, maybe even outrunning myself. Certainly I was outrunning any connection or identity that related to god, being a Christian, or the like. In college and for a while after graduation, I fought hard in Christian chat rooms (remember when those were a thing?) to be heard and seen, spending hours at night vehemently defending myself and others: *Yes, we can be gay and Christian, too!* The discussions never ended well, though, and I always left feeling worse than I had when I began. After my family outed me to the wider community, and things felt like they would never be the same with them or with any of my friends from church growing up, some part of me died inside. Some part of my faith died, too.

I suppose I was hoping, in those frenetic nighttime Internet arguments, that if I could convince a bunch of strangers that I could be both saved and queer, then somehow I could convince my own family. It would be years before I finally learned that you cannot convince other people. All you can really do is live your life by the "clarity of your own example," as Abraham-Hicks says, and pray for a few people who will truly see and know you. In the hard times when you are surrounded only by those who can't, you can still find—or at least work toward—peace within your own heart. We can't make folks accept us, love us, believe us, or see that we are a masterpiece. The only thing we can ever do is see that in ourselves.

In that early time, however, right after the painful explosion of energy that had taken place in my own world, I was far from being able to grasp this. I existed then in a fear-filled state, feeling that all the work I was doing to survive was never enough to heal my wounds, to fill the void I so desperately wanted to fill.

There is a fire that burns inside all of us, a fire for knowing, seeking out, and discovering our hopes and our true selves—where we came from and belong. When this fire is stoked with fear rather than faith, it can become an untenable force within us with the capacity to hijack our lives. It's a dangerous path, the steep, slippery road where our fear leads us. It can contain intense illnesses and depressions, unbalanced drug uses, other addictions and compulsions of many types, and hate-filled stances toward life and others in it.

For me, the process was deceiving, because in that fear-filled space, I quickly became attached to certain ideas and ideologies that made me feel safe and justified. In my case, I began operating as though everyone was against me, or out to get me. I told stories to myself and others that reinforced these ideas, and before long, they became my reality. Having once bought into these kinds of fears, nothing was easier than to lash out at others in anger, push people away when they attempted to get close to me, and try to isolate myself from pain by isolating myself from the world.

My depression had worsened and essentially taken over; I also developed such tremendous anxiety around leaving the house that I became nearly agoraphobic. It felt unbearable to be out in the world. My chronic stomach illnesses, too, took a terrible toll.

Living this way—hounded by fear, up to my neck in anger—felt almost comfortable. At the very least, it was familiar; it was all I knew how to do. But unbeknownst to me, I was traveling further down the spiral, growing more and more separated and distant from my true self—the precise opposite effect from the one I wanted.

•••

To navigate this world, and our struggles, we need something to guide us. We need a way to find our direction. We need a compass. And in those raw early years after coming out, that was precisely what seemed broken in me: my compass.

Those who have seen the *Pirates of the Caribbean* movies might remember Captain Jack Sparrow's compass. For those who haven't, a brief explanation: The protagonist Jack Sparrow, a pirate and endearing scoundrel, carries with him a compass that *doesn't* point to true north. Others tease him constantly about his broken compass. But over the course of the movies, something surprising happens. Along with other characters of the movies, you, as an observer, begin to notice something truly extraordinary. The compass isn't actually broken at all. It just points to something even more important than true north.

It points to what Jack desires most.

Granted, some scenes make this a joke; one movie's ending has him rowing in a tiny rowboat and opening the compass as the music crescendos, expecting it to point him toward his next big adventure. Instead, it points to his other hand, which is holding a bottle of rum. Only after he's taken a big swig does the compass shift direction off into the horizon.

But rum-based humor aside, as I watched these movies, I began to feel a longing for a compass like that—something that pointed in the direction of what I wanted, revealing what next steps I should take. The irony, of course, was that I already had such a compass; every one of us is born with one inside of us. That compass is the voice of the god within. But mine, like so many of ours, had been cast aside, labeled as broken, and accused of being untrustworthy.

Just as Jack Sparrow's fellow movie characters ridicule his "broken" compass, the world ridicules ours. From our very early years, we are told we don't know what's best. We are told everything to do and everything *not* to do. As we grow into small children and go to school, we are increasingly told to set aside our unique traits and individualized knowing and instead to conform—conform to these rules, these ways of being, the ideas and ideals of the teacher and the school. *Put away your compass*, we are told. *It's no good here.* Our families strongly enforce or "encourage" us to conform to their own patterns and rules. For many of us, this process happens in other places as well: religious communities, school, our places of work, and even other relationships we engage in. All of these spaces represent layers of stripping away our inner knowing, being taught to follow the north that's true for someone *else*, putting away that silly broken compass we have.

With time and pressure, like rocks dashed by wave after wave, we are molded and broken down, and we conform. We throw away or lose touch with our own compass. Reclaiming that compass is one of the hardest, most rewarding tasks our lives will give us.

At that time of my life, however, all I knew was that I was living without mine. My faith community and family had combined to cut my connection to it. Of course not all Christianity, nor all religion, has this effect, but sometimes it *really does*. Many people who have left the church, especially queer folks, report this as an ongoing issue we have faced. And for me, it was proving one of the hardest traumas of Christianity to heal.

Much of spirituality teaches how important it is to truly love yourself and to see yourself as inherently valuable and worthy. But what do you do when nearly everything and everyone in your life has reinforced your lack of value? When I look back on my struggling self of that time, I marvel at the obstacles I and others like me face when we try to reclaim our compasses. Within my church's teaching that we were all sinners, the message was implanted in my earliest child-self that I *wasn't* worthy, that I was inherently bad and flawed, and that there was nothing I could ever do to actually "fix" or "redeem" myself. Nothing inside of me was trustworthy. Only something outside of me—a white dude with a beard sitting on a throne on a cloud—could fix the problem of *me*.

No wonder I was lost, hurting, without direction. No wonder my mind and body were ill. When you add to my religious past the broader societal issues around gender, sexuality, and the like, the situation was compounded into such complexity and challenge that to this day I find it amazing that I'm still here, in my forties. The suicide rates within the LGBTQIA+ community are sadly high and also sadly unsurprising.

●●●

The strange thing about struggle is how often it lives side by side with growth—even joy. While all this trauma and turmoil was churning inside me, in my external life I was also finding new connections and having new horizons opened to me, as I came to know and belong to the queer community. Anya and I lived in the New England area for several years and made a lot of friends. I can say without hesitation that my ex-wife was my rock during my worst years. When my parents weren't around much, and other family members and friends had quit talking to me, she was there. She was so steady and loving. She was strong; she honestly kept us both afloat for so many years. I know without a shadow of a doubt that I wouldn't be here without her. When you have chronic illness and debilitating mental health issues, your partner often bears the brunt of it. Sometimes the ghosts of my past and my fear of the future completely consumed my present. She didn't always get the best of me, and amazingly, she stuck by me even in the lowest of times. May we all be blessed with loved ones who love us so fiercely, through our darkest hours, that we might find a way to love ourselves back into living. Of course, sometimes the amazing and incredible, steady and generous love from another person is not enough; sometimes overcoming isn't a reality. There are times when depression, addiction, or trauma are terminal diseases.

I was fortunate that my entrance into the queer community happened with a caring person like Anya at my side. It began the night I met Dorris, my current wife, at a concert. It was the night after George Bush was elected for a second term, in 2004. Dorris walked out onto a stage opening for the Indigo Girls, and I was enamored. (With her *music*, of course.) Anya and I both were. We began following her band around New England, seeing them play show after show, eventually meeting the band and becoming friends with them. This experience changed my entire world. Up until then, I had only known and been friends with straight people and cis people. But this band—they were different. Several of them identified as queer, and one person who worked with the band was even trans. I was starstruck—not only because they were talented musicians, but because I suddenly knew: *These could be my people.* I hadn't known that it was an option to just live out loud, so fully in the world.

Dorris and I became friends, and very quickly her friendship came to have a large impact on me. When we met, she was dating the trans guy who worked with the band—who was the first trans person I had ever met (at least to my knowledge back then, which was admittedly limited!). I was stunned. I kept thinking to myself, *I didn't know that was an option.* One day, in conversation with Dorris, she paused and looked at me. "Do you think you'd ever want to go by *he*?" she asked.

My mind ground to a halt. I fumbled for words. "That would be the last straw for my parents," I finally managed to say.

She smiled a little. "That didn't really answer the question," she said gently.

But I couldn't answer it—not that day. After everything exploded with my parents, for years there was nothing but strain, silence, and pain between us. A gradual settling down took place by about 2009; at one point, I even went home and stayed with them for a whole week, which I had not done since my senior year of college. The ceasefire felt like such a relief that I didn't want to push the envelope further. So I ignored Dorris's question, and it stored itself somewhere in my mind to be saved for a later day.

At that time, however, it was enough simply to be inaugurated into the queer community. As I followed Dorris's band over the coming years, I met so many more people like me: people who experienced the world in a different way; people who weren't afraid to be themselves; people who had pride in who they were, who lived without shame. It was foreign to me, but I felt so drawn to it, almost as if I was coming home.

By the mid-2000s, my partner and I had moved all the way across the country to California. The Bay Area was an entirely new experience yet again, another form of coming home. The entire area was filled with LGBTQIA+ people—miraculous! I became friends with a multitude of new people, with different backgrounds, religions, races, gender expressions, and identities. And while my depression, grief, illness, and heartache continued to be present, I also had many good days with my partner and all these new folks who had been brought into my life and with whom I began to form new communities. Family, I came to learn, wasn't limited to the people you were related to; family could be entirely created, ultimately chosen, and that, more than anything, began to ease some of my deep pains.

And meanwhile, I was still searching for my compass, my life's direction, the path to what I truly desired.

I decided to look at potential graduate school programs, and I stumbled upon a master's program in social change and justice. It was a small private school in San Francisco. I applied immediately, had a good interview, and entered the program the following fall.

I soon found myself in classrooms with such diverse mixes of people—more diverse, really, than any experience in my life thus far. The community was, at first, amazing, and I did meet some folks there who have been friends ever since. But something else happened there, something unexpected. These folks were all very liberal—the most liberal folks I'd ever been around. In fact, they made me look like a moderate. In the midst of several classes, I began to notice something; namely, that the far, far right and the far, far left were not all that different. Their fundamentalist ideas isolated them, in their minds, as the only ones who were correct, thus leaving everyone else in the wrong. That energy wasn't how the *whole* school was, by any means, just a handful of people; but it was enough to unsettle me. It felt all too familiar.

As school wrapped up that year and I headed into summer, I was wondering, *Is this for me? Is social justice work and fighting for LGBTQIA+ rights really something I can spend my life doing?* I'm sure you've been there yourself, unsettled, wanting to take the opportunity to reevaluate the next steps.

And sometimes, the universe seems to decide that on our behalf.

Not long after, the universe answered this question for me. In June, news started buzzing around the school that the program was in danger. The whole school was, in fact. As it turned out, an administrator had embezzled federal loan money. The school quickly filed for bankruptcy and shut down.

I was devastated. Here I was again, so newly come into my queer identity, and a community I had built was dispersed again. Gone. What now? I walked away with a load of student debt, 20-some credits shy of a master's degree. The credits I did have were essentially useless, non-transferable, because no one wanted to touch anything or anyone connected to that school.

Directionless, depressed, and lonely, I retreated into myself and felt my chronic health issues explode again. My mental health was bad enough, but the constant stomach and digestion issues felt never-ending and equally debilitating. In so many ways, my faith— the god within, my compass—felt entirely dead. Gone. Buried. Without that fuel for the fire of my life, all that burned was fear.

And the only thing holding the fear back...was the weed.

•••

A friend had recommended that I obtain a medical marijuana card, assuring me that with my health issues, I'd have no problem getting one. They were right. I started smoking weed, and holy *shit*, did that change everything. It really began to take the edge off. I quickly found my way into the world of medical dispensaries, beginning to learn what types of marijuana would help with what symptoms. In no time, there were improvements to my health. My aches and pains were not as extreme. Weed also lessened my fears of just being out in the world. It helped, at least somewhat, my stomach cramping and consistent digestive issues. It dulled my anxiety. It didn't cure anything, but it definitely gave me a boost and helped me to find some rest from everything.

My journey with cannabis went on like that for a few years. The depression still hit hard every winter, but that seemed to be something I couldn't fix no matter what I tried. *At least I'm feeling other relief*, I thought. *I'll take it.* Deep, genuine relief. It felt like a miracle.

And for quite a long time, it was. Until it wasn't.

I started to get in with groups of friends I wouldn't normally have connected with, just because we were all weed smokers. On one such occasion, a couple of these folks started talking about how they did meth on Saturdays to clean their house. I felt untethered, afraid, suddenly realizing I didn't recognize the people I was surrounding myself with—or even myself.

My day-to-day life and most of my relationships didn't suffer particularly. I was what we call a functional stoner. But within me, things progressed and began to feel out of control. When I was forced to be sober, I was aggravated, lashing out at people, completely short-tempered and angry at the world. I picked fights. I lost sight of myself.

Perhaps that shouldn't have come as a surprise to me—to lose sight of myself. Who was I, anyway? Did I know? Had I fully been able to tear down all the programming I was taught—to tear down the house, studs and all, and to actually rip out the foundation?

The answer, I discovered, was *no*.

I had torn down *part* of my house—that is, my family's and faith community's beliefs—ripping out the walls, the studs, the pipes. But then I tried to rebuild a new house on the same foundation, and I ended up, in a way, right back where I started. We all do this. It's natural. When we're taught to discard our desires, taught that our guidance system is faulty, and that in order to be safe, good, and happy, we must follow some external guidance system, then it's deeply understandable when we just replace one system with another, instead of embarking on the wild, risky, beautiful work of learning to live by our own inner compasses. That master's program experience had given me unexpected glimpses into my old life and my old people, who were only interested in their way or the highway.

And what was my way?

Who was I?

I had no idea. And I didn't know how to find him.

•••

Around that time, a therapist told me, "Sometimes you're in a well, and the only tool you have is a shovel. In that situation, you need to be capable of two things. One, you have to realize that that tool isn't going to solve the problem. And two, you have to be willing to put it down."

I didn't know then that I needed to tear down my house *again* and pull out the entire foundation. Building from the ground up was the only way back to myself and my heart's compass. And yet...I still hadn't hit rock bottom. Would I heed the warning of my therapist? Would I quit digging, put down my shovel, and then ask, "Now how the hell do I get myself out of the depths of this well?"

Not yet, I wouldn't. Not by a long shot.

●●●

Life's struggles, as I told you earlier, rarely happen without goodness right there within them. During this time of smoking weed, I was able to open up my heart to new experiences that I had long since sworn off—specifically, any connection to "god" or spirituality. Somehow, the weed enabled me to go to these deeper places, to re-encounter the spiritual nature that had been hijacked by others but that had always held great life-giving energy potential for me. As we approach the apocalypse time in my story, and as you contemplate such moments in your own stories, I invite you to notice the goodness that sustains us amid the chaos of this dense Earth of ours.

We have all experienced the struggle, the striving, the pain and suffering of this world. Yet often all it takes is a bit of openness within us, an unlocking that helps us begin to be open to the idea of remembering who we are. It starts small: one seed planted, and enough goodness to keep it alive, through our apocalypse times and all the way into our reemergence.

Dear beloved, unbound self, this is what I want to tell you...

Though you are in struggle, you do not have to be constrained and confined by every single thing in your experience. You have created this space within you where you are restrained, tied up, bound to outcomes of the most difficult sort. You have manifested yourself into this world, this experience, picturing yourself as a creature at the mercy of it all. But there is another path.

Today is the day to release yourself, to emerge from the constraints you've created around yourself. Choose freedom. You humans spend so much of your time trying to escape your circumstances, numbing out with whatever you can. Whatever it is for you—food, drugs, alcohol, sex, shopping, distraction after distraction—whatever you use, we promise you one thing: It's not working, and it isn't helping you feel better. Freedom is what you seek. Freedom is what you all seek.

You hold each other captive, too. You tell each other whom you can love and whom you can marry, who deserves the best jobs because of perceived "betterness," like the color of your skin, your socioeconomic path, the fitness or beauty of your body, or your gender. All of this must stop. You must choose to cease this part of your experience. None of you can be free if any one of you is still held captive.

Each of you reading this can create the space for this freedom as you practice holding the highest vision for this, knowing that oneness is what brings you all—us all—together. Remember that the struggle is not hopeless or useless. This is what you all came here in this lifetime to unleash. Your work is no longer about someone outside of yourself—the government, an authority figure, parents, etc.—telling you what is best for you and for everyone else. This is now the time for stepping forward with faith in your inner guidance: the god within, your highest self.

Many of you have lost sight of that compass; your divine direction seems lost in the mist or fog, somewhere far off in the distance. But it never leaves you. It's time to dust off that inner compass, close out the voices of the outside world that have been screaming at the top of their lungs at you and everyone else, and just grow quiet and listen. Listen for that still, small voice inside you; it's there, we promise. Even if you think it's not, or think it's gone, it is right there, and it always has been.

You will come to feel this yourself the more you practice slowing down, getting still, and getting off the gerbil wheel. The rat race is literally draining your soul. So, step off, quiet your heart and your mind, and just take some moments each day to actually listen. Don't talk, don't request, don't do anything; just be. Be in the moment, right where you are. Be open, not closed off and protected. Be available; listen with your heart. This, we promise you, will bring you back to your compass, showing you your divine direction. As you see it more and more clearly, you will be able to act from the place of knowing and heart-centered action. This is the only way to actually get anywhere. Otherwise, you just keep going around the gerbil wheel—around and around the same experiences until at last you learn the lessons and take a new, divinely guided path in the right direction.

This life is a wild and crazy ride sometimes. We know this. You knew it, too, going into this experience; that's why you chose it. The transformation is priceless, and it is something you truly cannot experience without the fire or the tsunami or the winds.

You are the Earth, as it is transformed by the other elements. Surrender, stop fighting, be within it. Be made anew, brought to life in a new way.

This is what you were seeking. We promise.

Dear Beloved writing prompt

Ask the god within to guide you in these questions: What do you have to tell me about learning to reach toward my own heart's compass? What can you show me about where in my life I am spinning, or grasping onto a shovel that I need to put down? How can I slow down?

Write down the response: "Dear beloved...."

CHAPTER FOUR

THE APOCALYPSE

*"In three words I can sum up everything
I've learned about life. It goes on."*
—Robert Frost

Most of us live rushing, hurrying, pushing, striving—until something brings us up short. Sometimes we are running *from* something; other times, we are seeking something that feels missing. We chomp at the bit to do the next thing, get the newest electronics, move somewhere new, make a new friend, find a new relationship, or start a new job.

Often we try to fill what feels missing through relationships. What feels missing is different for each of us, and that sense of separateness that the ego impresses upon us takes a unique shape in each person's life, but ultimately, the experience of feeling separate and lacking is universal. We long to feel that oneness and connection with our higher selves, with the god within us that we always feel separate from, somehow. In my case, some of this separation came from Christianity and its teaching that humans are sinners who mess up all the time—and so badly—that we need a savior. Others of us encounter separateness differently. But no matter where that feeling comes from, we often find ourselves looking for a savior of sorts—one person, one thing, or one relationship that can bring us the peace, salvation, healing, or purpose that we seek.

For me, relationships were always something I was seeking. I had grown up in a large family, including not only our relatives but also all sorts of guests bustling in and out of our house. My parents were always taking in someone who needed extra help, or having large gatherings and get-togethers. My brother and I regularly had groups of people over. Our house was a revolving open door. So when I left that home, and my new experience of "home" was just me and my partner, that was hard for an extrovert bred on extroverting. In those years following my coming out, I never stopped seeking out friends and family, trying to make connections, looking desperately for something that I couldn't even name.

When our state of being is one of desperate seeking, we begin to realize something: All the things, people, and relationships we try never quite give us the "thing" we are looking for. For a while, perhaps, we discover something that soothes or excites us, or someone who gives us the sense of being filled, of belonging—but that feeling of being "filled up" doesn't last. The energy exchange is like a sieve; we fill up only to have it drain right back out in what can feel like a very short amount of time. My own experience with this sieve-like energy exchange made up a large part of my struggle with depression—as I suspect it does for many of us. It makes sense: If many things that you try fill you up and give you a sense of relief, but then suddenly the flood gates open and everything drains back out, that's a cycle of finding only to lose that can cause terrible frustration, even grief. Sometimes we end up feeling that we don't want to keep being in this world.

Dear beloved, I urge you again not to worry. This drive to fill ourselves up, to belong, to be in connection and be made whole again, is natural. Every single person on the planet has felt this energy and has sought after it in one way or another, even if they can't admit it. And it's okay that some things work for a while and then fade away into the distance, like a car we pass and gradually watch growing smaller in our rearview mirror. This, too, is natural, not a sign that you're doing something wrong. And I have one more spoiler alert for you: This experience of each thing coming and then going, seeping out through the sieve? If we let it, this very experience will take us one step closer to the essence of our pain— and how we can begin to heal it. And even more, this longing, this neediness that we all have, is actually something that can unite us. It shows us how alike we are, far more alike than we often realize. It takes us places we need to go, brings us to people we need to meet, and gradually, over time, shows us what we need to know.

But I won't give you the answer to the root of this longing—not yet. After all, we are still in the midst of the struggle, and the answer to the longing only comes in the emergence that lies ahead.

●●●

In the late 2000s, as my struggle came to a head, I became increasingly more chaotic within. It was like I couldn't get enough. I couldn't get enough time with the people I wanted to be around.

I couldn't get enough food, so I ate more and more. I couldn't get enough weed, so I bought more and smoked more, over and over again. I couldn't get enough attention or touch, so I kept seeking out more in ways that weren't always healthy for me. I couldn't get enough love, ultimately—or at least, that's how my brain had translated all those things that filled me. In pursuit of connection, I often put myself last and tried to do things for everyone else. My buddy Nate used to say to me, "You would drive to Alaska for a friend if they needed something." That was absolutely accurate, but it wasn't always the best thing for me. So many things—relationships, drugs, boundaries, and more—had become extremely out of balance in my life. But I didn't have the first clue as to how to find my way into greater balance.

For years, I sat on the outside looking in on Dorris's life, into her band and her friends, almost worshipfully gazing at this amazing group of people that I saw living their lives and their truths unafraid or unashamed. I desperately, hungrily wanted in on that. More and more, I wanted *her*, and everything she represented in my mind: freedom, healing, joy, wholeness.

Dorris became the first person I opened back up to, about five years after the fallout with my family. I don't mean that I wasn't close to Anya and even other people; sure, I made friends—I'm an extrovert, I can't not! I talk to everyone, in grocery stores (or any store, for that matter), in lines, at work, you name it.

I always made friends, but there is a difference between being casual friends or work friends—even being partners who live together—and having a level of intimacy where you

go deeply beyond your persona, your mask: the self that the
outside world sees when they look at you, and even the self
you are used to seeing when you look in the mirror. You could
say that intimacy isn't just when we show someone who you
are; it's when you show someone who you might become.

When you dig down to the roots of who you *might* be if you do
the work and actually allow yourself to unfold in new ways, and
you let someone else witness and share in this with you, the kind
of intimacy that emerges is unlike any other. I have come to call
this "spiritual intimacy." At this level of intimacy, I could talk about
my beliefs about god and the universe, love, energy, spirit guides,
modalities that I had come across, books I had read, classes I'd
taken, readings I'd had, where I thought these things could take
me, and on and on.

Dorris and I went to that level together—naturally, as though we
were both speaking the same mother tongue. She was so easy to
talk to; she made me feel unafraid of being vulnerable and sharing
all the stories that, up until then, I had kept under wraps with any
new people I met. Dorris was only the second person, and the first
person in my "new life," whom I told in full detail about the young
man who died of AIDS after my mom told him he would burn in
hell. I told her about my struggle with losing god; I told her how,
in some ways, I had come to hate god (or so I thought at the time).
We would spend countless hours on the phone together, staying
up until all hours of the night, talking as endlessly as teenagers.

Anya and I had been together for years by that time, and we had
known each other in our even younger years as friends, but we

also had had to deal with what had happened in our lives—and how folks responded to our relationship—in our own individual ways. Now, I can't speak for her, but on my part, I learned that a partner can't be everything to us. They can't fulfill all the needs we have. This is normal and by design. So, although Anya and I were close and loved one another, our lives were unfolding differently; my passion and appetite for spiritual intimacy needed to be filled with other people and not just within our relationship.

As a teenager, I had so many different groups of friends, and a handful of best friends—not just one or two, but as many as five or six at times. Some were from school and sports teams, but most came from church. I shared that deep spiritual intimacy with them, telling them what I truly thought and felt about the most profound things in life. So when that all disappeared, almost instantaneously, in the aftermath of the explosion of coming out, it took me years to feel willing to ever go there again, to share spiritual intimacy with anyone.

While I was avoiding that spiritual intimacy, I didn't realize I was experiencing it as a lack; but as I grew closer to Dorris (and to her bandmate Nate), I knew that I wanted more spiritual intimacy in my life again. Though Anya supported and loved me, it became gradually clearer that I wanted more in that area than our relationship had to offer. Our interests and focus began to diverge, which wasn't wrong or bad; we had simply begun to naturally outgrow our relationship (and, ultimately, each other). My life was moving toward new directions that didn't always include her, and the same was true of her life. Somehow, perhaps because she and I had lived through that shared coming-out crisis together, she wasn't the person who could help me find god again. It had to be someone else entirely—someone not tied to that life or even that *me*.

And that someone turned out to be Dorris. I couldn't seem to resist going there with her, sharing that intimate, spiritual space, and the same was true for her as well. We saw the god within each other and thus saw the face of god through our interactions. In the midst of that relationship, I realized how deeply I had missed seeing the face of god in others. And I knew then that I wanted more of that.

No matter how close Dorris and I became, I always wanted more. The possibility of having that spiritual intimacy return to me, of seeing the deep face and love of god in new people again, felt like coming alive after being entombed for so long; no wonder I was eager for more. But at the human level, that eagerness, that hunger, often manifested as pressure: pressure for our relationship to *be more*. She knew it. Her partner at the time knew it. Our friends knew it. It was no secret. I think even Anya knew it. But I don't think others always understood what the *more* was that I wanted. Over time, I did begin to feel the desire to be with her in a romantic way, but I also just craved the spiritual intimacy. At times, I felt like that might be enough, though I wasn't always sure it would be.

Dorris, however, felt a discomfort around the question of *more* for her. She wasn't sure she wanted anything more than our spiritual intimacy always assured me that a romantic relationship was never happening. She'd tease me from time to time, declaring, "I have *zero* attraction to you." With my lack of self-esteem, I simply believed that, but I also had moments of knowing—in my heart, but also with my seeing and intuitive ways—that there was something more there between us.

The trouble is, sometimes we fall in love with the idea of who someone is—or even the idea of who we might be if we were with them.

Enchanted with this vision, we don't take the time to look at what's "missing" underneath all that. We think being with them might solve all our problems—the same way we might think that having a baby could save a relationship, or that getting a new job would make life feel new, or that moving to a new place would automatically create the fresh start we want to have. The truth is, all too often, the things that burdened us before will just be carried over into that new space—the new parenthood, the new romance, the new job, the new city—unless we really do the work around what we need to heal. Instead, we overlook or don't attend to the parts of our current reality, or our current selves, that actually make that vision impossible or unrealistic. We don't truly grapple with the hard work we'd need to do in order to bring that vision into the world. When I watched Dorris, and felt the way I did around her, I wanted to be in her world; I wanted so badly to be *already there*: at my true self, with her at my side.

But the truth was, we both needed to do a lot more work before we would be ready to be together in that way. For myself, I had yet to fully enter and work with the desperation I felt, the ravenous *wanting more* that was driving me deeper into addiction and unbalanced life choices. I still wanted something or someone "out there" to save me from my pain—from my history—from my confusion and fear—in other words, from my own life.

● ● ●

For many years, I cycled through a predictable depression that revolved around (oddly enough) baseball season. From March to October, I often managed to stay a little more grounded and in less despair, although that wasn't always the case. But once baseball season ended and the shorter days of winter really set in, my depression set up camp and moved in for the long off-season.

2012 was another long and dreary winter filled with depression and deep isolation. The colder months seemed to last longer and longer. I yearned for the springtime to return; something about that season often changed my heart space. Remember all the Mayan folklore saying that the world was ending in 2012, the movies and the prophecies about such dramatic destruction? Well, the world stuck around, but I felt that shift energetically; it was as though something in me had come to an end. I certainly felt like I might be destroyed. My personal apocalypse was beginning.

● ● ●

In the last few weeks of 2012, Dorris and I had an explosive fight. At the time, I was still a serious pot smoker; I had in fact spent a good portion of the previous four years smoking. The addiction played a huge role in the destruction of my relationship with her, with other people, and inside myself, but obviously I couldn't see that at the time. They say that those who are drowning sometimes work themselves into such a panic that they take their would-be rescuers down with them. I didn't know it at the time, but this was the energy I began bringing to Dorris. And there came a point when, for her own life's sake, she had to remove herself from my reach. That was the last thing I wanted—and the very thing I did not know I needed most.

Dorris at last had to step away from me. My need had become too desperate, my energy too out of balance, for her to feel secure being as close to me as she was. Her stepping away—partially, during this first apocalypse event, and then entirely, during the second one—ultimately saved our relationship, but at the time all I felt was heartbreak. The strain between us seemed only to confirm my worst fears that I was fundamentally broken and not good enough.

Our ego thrives on such seeming "confirmations" of our worst fears. It leaps into high gear, continuing to tell the stories that we think have kept us safe. *You see? I knew no one could be trusted. I knew everyone always leaves and abandons me. I'm not worthy of love. I will never belong. I'm not enough. I'm broken beyond repair. My needs will never be met.* But in reality, those stories don't keep us safe. They keep us small, and suffering, and isolated, and stuck.

Sometimes, it takes literally losing someone or something precious to finally pry ourselves loose from the grip this "stuck" part has on us, and to realize that it is no longer serving us. Our loss plunges us deeper, chiseling away yet another layer of the parts of ourselves that are inhibiting our growth and our access to the best and highest good for us. Though I've regained a lot of the relationships I have lost over the years, they all have come back in new forms and with new boundaries—even limitations. But they serve me better than they did before, when I was simply holding on to people because I was ultimately afraid of being abandoned.

At the time, however, all I could feel was misery, rage, panic, and suffering. The first apocalypse event had come. Dorris and I were on the outs, and I did not know the way forward.

●●●

I'm on the plane home from Atlanta to the Bay, raw and miserable from the fight with Dorris, and on top of it I have a terrible, excruciating tooth infection. Arriving home, I feel like I have a terrible flu plus the most intense jaw pain and toothache that I have ever felt in my life.

Finally I get to a dentist, who tries to work on it and discovers that the infection has already spread too deep. The only recourse is to pull the tooth, and I have to wait for an available surgery date.

Nothing, but nothing, touches the pain: not antibiotics, nor prescription painkillers, nor the highest-quality weed. One night, the pain is so bad that I pass out from it.

The day of the surgery finally comes, and I'm sitting in the surgeon's chair, reading the paperwork. I come across this instruction in large font: "YOU CANNOT SMOKE DURING THE NEXT TWO WEEKS!"

I almost drop the paperwork. I'm mouth-wide-open stunned.

For a long, long moment, I consider getting up and walking out. *Nothing's controlling the pain—not prescription drugs and not the weed—but...two whole weeks without it....* Eventually I realize that I simply cannot bear this pain any longer; I have no other choice. The infection could spread to my bloodstream otherwise, and who knows what would happen then? So...I stay.

• • •

Afterward, sober for the first week in as long as I could remember, I was struggling, to say the least. In some sense, there are no words to actually express the struggle unless you yourself have lived this. Coming out of the often-wonderful fog of daily weed use, back into facing the "real" world, was the rudest awakening I could have imagined. On top of it, I felt intense shame about having let my attachment to weed get that far. How could something that had started as such an amazing and helpful tool have become a crutch that I feared I couldn't live without?

In the years since, I have slowly learned that this is simply how we travel through life. All the things that we think we have lost, or that feel like they have been taken from us, are in fact just tools that were no longer useful to us. We are allowed to need these tools, for a time; we are allowed to lose them and grieve their loss; and in time, we come to be able to let go of them and embrace what new tools we find. I didn't need to punish myself for that. None of us do.

Christianity, my childhood version of god, was useful to me in this way, and then it came time for me to let it go. And I did take some meaningful things from my time with Christianity about who I am in the world. My parents taught me to be loving and kind, to help your neighbors, to be a servant, and to have a big heart. Those are all parts of myself that I still carry with me today, even though I might not use the same wording or tie them to the same roots that my folks did. In the same way, I would eventually grow out of the terrible shame over my addiction and become able to see the weed as a tool that was no longer what I needed in order for my best and highest good to come to fruition. It wasn't wrong or bad when I needed it, and it wasn't wrong or bad when it was no longer in my best interest. My time with it had simply come to an end.

The endings of relationships, even though those can be the most traumatic of experiences, can work the same way, eventually leading to greater health. Though Dorris had not yet cut ties with me, our relationship was rocky, no longer something I could lean into in the way I had been doing. But I couldn't acknowledge or adaptively respond to that reality yet. Instead, I kept on pressing for more, trying to get back somehow to where we had been— even though neither of us *could* go back. I was terrified, in pain, feeling as though my life and my own self had become more than I knew how to handle—or even to endure—and that now, I had to face it all without the person who had become my lifeline: the one who had become the face of god to me, and my way to the god within.

These were my first excruciating steps into sobriety: taking responsibility for my own life and well-being, and beginning to truly grow up into the person I would become. In those first months, the only thing I could muster up the strength to do was to dive more deeply into my spiritual work. As I did, I began to change inside. This process will be unpacked in greater detail in Part III, but in short, I began uncovering my deeper truths, and it became evident that I couldn't keep existing as I had.

One realization that emerged from this work was that I could no longer stay in the Bay Area. It had served me—just like the weed, just like everything else—but now it was time to move on. Even though it had felt like home, I knew that my sobriety required a change of pace. I've always had an "itch" after a few years in a place, a feeling that it is time to leave. We had spent seven years in the Bay Area already; it was time.

Later that year, Anya and I headed for Austin, Texas. We had quite a few friends living there, including my best friend from high school; she and I hadn't lived near each other since we were 17. So, I figured: *Why the hell not?*

During and after the move, I kept reminding myself, "Sure, it's Texas...but it's Austin." Some days that was enough; other days it wasn't. Again, as in times before, my early transition to the new place was fairly easy and enjoyable. New things hadn't led to routines yet; the excitement of new places and friends pushed down my ever-present mental health challenges and my struggle with new sobriety (as well as health issues that recurred upon getting sober). Anya and I grew very close during that time.

But eventually, life became routine again; Anya got a job and went back to work full time. Friends who had initially been so excited to have this time with us got busy with other things as the newness wore off. And once more, I was left to my own devices, frequently alone. Since the late 2000s, I had been working from home. After college, I had worked at a few sales jobs and then, after a layoff, found work for a nonprofit as a temp. That later became full-time work, and after moving out to California, I began working for them as a consultant. The freedom this provided me came with pros and cons. I would not have been able to undertake master's work (or later, seminary work) without the flexibility this job gave me. But working five days a week alone at home, with minimal human interaction, is a difficult challenge for an extrovert. Once all the newness wore off in Austin, I was—you guessed it—quickly right back where I had been in the Bay Area. Alone most of the time, and aching for something. But for what? I still didn't fully know.

I continued to dig deeper into my own psyche, not knowing what other direction I might take. I began having intense panic attacks, to the point that one day I had to pull off the road and call Anya, almost certain she would need to come and pick me up. The sensations of visceral panic that day made me feel like I was having a heart attack; I had never endured panic that powerful or scary before. Eventually, I was able to calm myself down enough to get home, but at that moment, I knew that I needed to get back to therapy.

Therapy quickly made it clear that a large part of this anxiety and panic was rooted in a desire to unleash myself, to let myself be free as me. But I still wasn't sure what that even meant. The question Dorris had once asked, *Would you ever want to go by he?*, began resurfacing in my mind. By then, I had made forays into shamanism—don't worry, I promise we'll get there—that had further developed this question, but I had set all of that aside as if it had not made a huge impact on my being. With the apocalypse blasting me open, I began to revisit it. For the first time, I contemplated what it might look like to transition—what that even meant, really. I was terrified to push the boundaries of society and my family yet again. Could

I find some sort of compromise? Maybe just a breast reduction? Would that be easier on my family? No sooner would I consider this than I would drop into anxiety: What if I compromised myself out of fear, again? I may not have known what this apocalypse was bringing about in my life, but I certainly couldn't deny one truth it had already brought to the forefront: fear was ruling and wrecking my life.

But I still didn't know how to get out of it. All I knew was that I had hit rock bottom.

Funny thing about rock bottom: Sometimes you think you've gotten to it, and then something even more intense happens, and you drop down to a whole new level of what rock bottom actually is. I don't think this means our earlier experiences weren't rock bottom, or that we exaggerated; I think this is simply a manifestation of the truth that life comes at us in waves. Where the wave hits, where we are at the moment, determines a lot.

I had thought the tension and pain in my relationship with Dorris, the tooth infections—which kept recurring—and surgery, and the arduous process of getting sober, were rock bottom enough. But there was more to come.

●●●

It's the fall of 2014, and Dorris and I are still managing to maintain a connection, albeit a strained one. But we have another blowout fight. As I'm reeling from it, I get a text from her.

I don't think I can be friends with you anymore.

I call. No answer. I stammer to her voicemail, "I just wanted a chance to say goodbye. So many of my relationships have ended with no notice, no reason, and no goodbye." My voice breaks a bit. I try to breathe. "So...goodbye."

I am devastated. The winter depression hits especially hard. My heart is in pieces again, and the blows seem to keep coming.

●●●

Could I possibly get to the place where I might see my relationship with Dorris as a tool for growth that was no longer serving me? That would take some time, because in those initial months, I just felt heartbroken, facing winter within and without.

There were glimmers of light in my rock bottom. I had Anya's unwavering support, some of my new friends in Austin, and my best friend from high school, Alice, and I was growing more adept in some spiritual techniques that were new to me, expanding my awareness with sources of self-care and self-discovery like acupuncture, shamanic training, meditation, and intuitive readings. (There is more on all that in the next chapters.) Alice's amazing family, the Gerharts, had also moved down to the Austin area, and that was lovely, because they had been like a second family to me for decades.

Unfortunately, Alice's father was suffering from Alzheimer's, and it was becoming quite advanced. They had moved down there, in fact, to be closer to two of their kids and have more help. It felt nice to have some "family" around, even though it was certainly hard to see my surrogate father declining so rapidly. Some days he was lucid, and other days he was not. After I had come out and things had been so hard with my family, the Gerharts had always welcomed me with open arms. When Alice told them back in the early 2000s that I had come out, they said, "Good for her," with a deep sense of pride. They had been my family of choice.

Alice and I had always found our way back to one another no matter how much time had passed between talking or seeing each other. She was family, and so were her folks. So in early 2015, when her mom Creta was diagnosed with lung cancer, it hit us all like a ton of bricks. *This can't be happening*, I thought to myself. I had already lived through a cancer scare with Dorris five years earlier; thankfully, she came out of that okay. I wished we were still friends, that I could call her to talk to her about the diagnosis that my surrogate mom had received.

Over the coming months, Creta had treatments and eventually even surgeries that only seemed to make her sicker, not healthier. I couldn't understand how this was happening. In the late days of April, she passed away. Another important person in my life—another part of my family—gone.

●●●

The apocalypse had come, and it had passed through me, over me, laying me bare. I experienced it as a cataclysm, a tragedy, the end of my world—everything we usually mean by that word. But as it turns out, *apocalypse* is an old word, much older than any one person's story. In ancient Greek, its roots mean *to uncover, to unveil*. Mine unveiled a life ruled, regulated, limited, and infested by fear. It uncovered a great and terrible truth: I had to change. I could not go on like this.

I had given fear so much power over so many parts of my life. There was my childhood fear of hell, of punishment from god...my fear of my own desires and behavior...my fear of being alone, of being abandoned, of being cast out...and ultimately, there was the fear that facing my trauma, my emotions, and the depths of my own soul would be the end of me.

I faced all of this and more, always fearing, in some ways, both the known and unknown. Some of my fears came true; others did not. That I feared losing loved ones to cancer had not prevented some from dying and others from living. That I feared losing more people than I could count didn't stop me from losing some of them—nor from finding others along the way, nor from being reunited with some of those I had lost. What, in the end, was my fear doing for me? Life seemed to go on regardless.

I think about how, in the history of humanity, our fear of the unknown has never fully stopped us from exploring. We endeavor to attain new heights; we reach out into the unknown and encounter newness. Our ancestors traveled across huge continents and vast, unknown oceans to get to new places; they launched themselves in rocket ships into outer space. With no true knowledge of what was on the other side, they did it anyway.

Fear can be a driving source that pushes us to reach for more, but it can also be a freezing force that causes us to shut down and stand still. That latter one is a space that doesn't serve us. My apocalypse unveiled exactly where I was—so deeply beholden to my fear that it had frozen me, leaving me incapable of being the person I knew myself to be. It showed me a picture of myself I wanted to change.

I didn't want to go on as trapped by fear as I was. I wanted to learn to be curious and open to forging new paths, to see where the rocket ship might take me, or where the boat traversing the vast ocean might go.

What would it be like if I allowed myself to end up at new places with new knowledge and experience from the adventure? What would happen if I stepped back from the fear of the unknown and instead embraced the journey home, and the available lessons along the way?

That was the transitional period I was heading into next: a time to stop rushing, hurrying, and striving to get somewhere. A time in which I would become open and ready to connect once more. To my own surprise, I would soon learn that even though relationships end, even as we are constantly seeking something that feels missing, and even as life itself appears to end, all of it—somehow, by some mystery—goes on.

But first we have to live it.

Dear beloved, relationship-seeking self, this is what I want to tell you...

Everything in you that seeks out a romantic relationship is actually the soul part of you that is yearning to connect with its oneness again. In your soul, you are remembering, knowing, and experiencing that all is oneness; but because of how human experience works, things appear to be separated, distanced. You appear to be alone; the unhoused person on the street corner appears to be alone; the child abandoned by its parents appears to be alone. Aloneness is on constant display. So your movies and newspapers, your magazines and talk shows, all demonstrate to you the need to fill that void with a romantic relationship, suggesting through sheer repetition that this is the only way to fulfillment and connection.

But the reality is that all connections are fulfilling, when you approach them within the space of remembering your oneness. Connecting with someone at the grocery store for five minutes can deliver this fulfillment. And conversely, because the romantic partnership is so sought after, pressed for with such need and desire, the intense pressure for romance to "succeed" and live up to societal expectations makes it harder and harder to actually access fulfillment through it.

The same can be true for those of you who are already in romantic relationships, because you have "found the one." This can result in deep disillusionment, because oneness is larger than any single relationship. Sometimes this opens a space in which you forget to make the other connections, those society deems less important or less necessary. But you are also still working to reconnect all parts of yourself, to realign yourself with oneness and be unified in love.

Each experience can learn something from the other. Whether or not you are partnered currently, remember to also take the time to be open energetically to other connections throughout your daily experiences. Open your heart at the bank and connect with the teller; open your heart at the store, allowing connection to appear in whatever bits and pieces it so desires. Text an old friend you haven't spoken to in a while. Connect.

This connection is essentially what you are all seeking, and not because you don't have it—that's the confusion. It's not "missing" from your experience; it's never gone from you. You are never *not* connected. You are complete, whole oneness. You are united with all energy, which is the very core of what courses through each and every single entity on this planet, in the stars, and every galaxy, even expanding to include what is beyond your human comprehension.

We will say it again: you are never not connected. You are never truly isolated, alone, lost, or forgotten. No, beloved, you are not. And yes, we know that from your human perspective, that seems almost laughable to say—if it didn't make you want to cry, too. There are excruciating times in your human experience where everything feels so desolate and isolated that you feel you could just die of aloneness.

But we promise you, even in those darkest nights of the soul, during the times of the deepest aloneness you could experience, if you drop gently into faith and reach out through your feeling heart, you will sense connection—even if it's just to the chair you are sitting on, or the fire that's warming your house as you sit by it. Reaching further, you can call upon any energies you need to feel connection and love—from spirit animals, to angels, your ancestors, ascended masters, and all loved ones who are always with you.

Most deeply, you can reach within yourself. Picture a compass showing you 360 degrees of experience around you. At some point on your journey, you might look around and not be able to see anyone or anything to connect to. Yet even in those times, the compass always points somewhere. That is your point of connection. Even when you feel like all is void, there is a small inner voice calling you toward that sliver of compass that is pointing you home: home toward your true self, remembering you are the very essence of connection and can never be anything but. Home toward your divine direction, toward remembering who you are, where you came from, and why you are here.

Dear Beloved writing prompt

Ask the god within to answer these questions for you: How may I reach more deeply within myself to feel connection and oneness at the core of my being—how can I reach you more? How can I remember that even in my darkest hours, I am not alone?

Write down the response, beginning, "Dear beloved...."

What Needs to Be Said About the Struggle

"Every time you are tempted to react in the same old way, ask if you want to be a prisoner of the past or a pioneer of the future."
—Deepak Chopra

Your struggle is real. In the very moment that you are feeling it, it is real. Your feelings around it—what comes up for you in the midst of it—are 100 percent valid. If you've experienced life even remotely like I have, you probably haven't felt like you received much validation in your life. So take a moment, close your eyes, and breathe in a slight bit of relief, taking in the words, "My experience, my feelings—they are valid."

Now let's breathe into that more deeply, knowing we are ready to step beyond the struggle and look more closely at how to move through it and into a new place. Going deeper and looking more closely—coming to a new place with it—doesn't mean there won't be more struggle and strife ahead. There will be. But staying stagnant in *this* part of the struggle—one you've been facing for years or holding onto for a lifetime—likely isn't serving you anymore.

For better or worse (but I think better), I can't bring you out of your struggle. I can't wave a magic wand and say, "Do these exercises and your life will magically improve." Things don't work that way. Instead, we will simply take the next set of steps together and see what unfolds.

WHAT NEEDS TO BE SAID PRACTICE: DO THE OPPOSITE

For the first practice in this section, let's explore another opportunity to get in touch with your heart's compass—your Jack Sparrow compass. Many things block us from living fully in alignment with this compass, and we have already discussed a number of them. This time, we will be looking at the way our learned behavior gets in the way. By "learned behavior," I am referring to the way we pick up mannerisms, ways of talking, patterns of reacting, and habits of coping from those who raised us. In most cases, we picked these up unintentionally, very early on, and over many, many years. By the time we make it into adulthood, our learned behavior is running on autopilot. We are rarely even aware when we are doing it, and we usually don't see the patterns. We're baffled when the same issues and conflicts seem to keep recurring in our relationships, our workplaces, or our experiences out in the world, and often, we conclude something like: The world is an unfriendly place. People are out to get me. I always get knocked down like this. It's like I'm cursed never to be happy, never to succeed, never to get my needs met. Yet all the while, we may be cocreating what happens to us and remaining completely unaware of how our learned behaviors are playing a big role in bringing these repeated struggles into being. All of this knocks us out of balance with our heart's compass.

Some of our learned behaviors come with high price tags: exhaustion, resentment, broken or lost relationships, you name it. When we're suffering under the weight of these symptoms, we all too easily interpret them as the universe being cruel to us, maybe even especially cruel to us. We may see ourselves as singled out: How come other people are getting a free pass while we're being dealt this misery? We get stuck in a victim mentality and miss noticing the part we are playing in the emergence of these symptoms.

Ironically, that part we are playing is precisely where we have the most power to change what we are facing—to become pioneers of our future rather than prisoners of our past, as Deepak Chopra says. And that's where our practice comes in.

I built this practice as a means for attempting a work-around for patterns we have learned from other people that are no longer serving us. It's a deceptively simple practice, but as most of us know, simple and easy are not the same thing. This is an in-depth practice that takes real commitment to your mental health and overall well-being. You must be willing to decide that you are ready to move through your struggle—those patterns of suffering in your life that are all too familiar—and out of victimhood, into the unknown beyond that.

So what is this practice, and how does it work? In a nutshell, it is this:

Do the opposite.

Simple—but not easy. Let's walk through this process step by step, and then you can begin bringing this practice into your own life, working with your unique "stuck" places, your learned behaviors and the familiar suffering they bring.

1. **First step: Notice.**

   In some ways, this is the hardest part of the practice, because as I said, we are often unaware of our own learned behaviors. The first things other people notice about us—and complain about!—might be the things we are most ignorant of. When that is the case, and you don't know what learned behaviors to identify in yourself, try starting with the feedback you seem to keep getting from other people. Have people been trying to get you to "lighten up" ever since you can remember? Or the reverse: Are they always telling you that you need to take life more seriously, that you're too flighty and irresponsible? Have you been told you take things too personally, or that you're totally cold and uncaring? Have you been told you focus too much on the needs of other people and not enough on yourself? Or that you are selfish and often aren't a good listener or friend? What about being told that you're too much or too loud, or that you're too meek and don't stand up for yourself?

Repeated, similar feedback from different people throughout your life is usually a great indicator of a place where learned behavior might be at play. Try identifying just one type, and begin watching for its appearance. You will start to notice yourself in a situation that feels familiar, and you have this moment—almost like a moment of *déjà vu*—where you recognize: *I've been here before. This feels familiar.* Eventually you might recognize: *I normally respond in a certain way to this circumstance; I do one particular thing in response.* This is the moment to stop—notice—breathe.

And then do the opposite.

2. **Second step: Do the opposite.**

I'll offer an example from my own learned behavior practice. My brother and I often bicker; we always have, since we were small kids. *What* we're bickering about changes, but the *fact* that we're bickering never does. It's a cycle that always ends badly: in fist fights, yelling matches, foot-sized holes in doors that were slammed in someone's face, or all-out WWE wrestling matches.

One day, quite a few years ago now, I was riding in the car with him, and we started the bickering. Back and forth we went, barely needing to think, or even take a breath; we were both so used to this territory. Like a dance we'd learned by heart, we didn't have to give any thought to the steps. It just happened. Our angry words came rushing out, flashing back and forth between us. All of a sudden, it occurred to me: *Do the opposite.* So...I did. Instead of staying in the flow of bickering, I just closed my mouth and didn't respond. I didn't take the bait or push back. I didn't defend myself or raise my voice. I just sat in silence. After a few minutes, something miraculous happened. My brother sat quietly for a moment in the driver's seat and then looked at me and said, "Well, that's no fun anymore." The bickering stopped, just like that. It stopped because I started doing something different—not because I waited for him to start.

As you practice doing the opposite, make sure you take note of that important dynamic. We often think that we need others to behave differently, to change or adjust their patterns of behavior so that we can feel better.

We spend all kinds of emotional energy trying to get them to change and being furious or resentful when they don't. But in the end, the best chance you have of changing established patterns in relationships is by changing what you are doing.

When you notice your learned behaviors and do the opposite, that changes the energy of the entire situation. Though there are no guaranteed outcomes—other people make their own choices, after all—you will almost always get a different response from the other person. How could you not? The actual momentum, the entire situation, changes in that instant that you do the opposite.

To do the practice for yourself, I want you to take some time to sit down and write some examples from your own life. As we discussed earlier, find things that are repetitive: a struggle with a partner, parent, or friend; criticism you keep receiving; a person (maybe a coworker) whose behavior always irritates you; a string of relationship types that ended badly. The who doesn't matter. Just take time to come up with a few examples, and then write down what you normally do—how you normally react or respond. Finally, get creative and come up with an alternative, "do the opposite" reaction (or two) for each.

I promise you that if you practice this—doing the opposite in your imagination before you start doing it in real time—you will create a new muscle memory, a new learned behavior, and something will change in your life.

Now open your journal and make that list.

WHAT NEEDS TO BE SAID PRACTICE: GOOD? BAD? WHO KNOWS?

For our second practice in Part II: The Struggle, we will build on one we began in Part I: The Origin. In our "Reframing the Whys" practice, we focused chiefly on the energetic shift that happens in our hearts when we take the narrow "why" about things that have happened to us and change it to a broad why. The narrow whys are usually filled with blame—either blaming others or ourselves—and they bring up feelings of anger, fear, isolation, or despair. The broad whys, in contrast, feel warm, softer, more peaceful and centered. Whichever why we are telling, however, the deepest truth at play is that we rarely ever actually know the real why behind most of the things that happen to us.

Making peace with that truth can be quite difficult to do, and like all challenging things, it takes practice. So for our second exercise, we are going to embark on some practice in sitting with and embracing the uncertainty as we take our "reframing the whys" to a new level.

Our starting point is the following parable, one which I have heard told many times by many different people and teachers, often attributed to a Chinese storytelling tradition. The story goes something like this:

> Once upon a time, there was a woman who owned a farm. One day, she came home with a horse. Her neighbor came over and exclaimed, "What good fortune! You got a horse to help in your fields!"
>
> The farmer replied, "Good? Bad? Who knows?"
>
> Later, the horse broke out of its stall and ran away. Again, the neighbor came over to give his two cents. "Oh, no, what terrible fortune!"
>
> The farmer responded: "Good? Bad? Who knows?"
>
> Some time passed, and the horse returned—not alone, but with three other wild horses in tow! The neighbor ran over, proclaiming, "What a miracle of good fortune! Now you are rich, and your farm will grow exponentially!"
>
> And again, the farmer responded: "Good? Bad? Who knows?"
>
> Now the farmer's son decided to break the wild horses. One day, he was thrown from one of them and broke his

leg. Upon hearing of this, the nosy neighbor declared, "What terrible fortune! Now you have no one to help you work your fields."

Yet again, the farmer said simply, "Good? Bad? Who knows?"

Ultimately, a war broke out throughout the region, and soldiers came through the village, taking with them every young person who might be able to fight. Yet they could not take the farmer's son because of his broken leg. The neighbor, as you can guess, waxed eloquent about the astonishing good fortune of his friend the farmer, who alone among all her peers still had her child beside her.

The farmer, in her quiet wisdom, once more said, "Good? Bad? Who knows?"

Now, this story could go on endlessly, but I think you see the point. We have, in every moment and every circumstance, a choice to make about the meaning we assign to everything that happens. Is it good? Is it bad?

Or do we not know?

Hopefully you've practiced reframing the whys and are becoming comfortable with that. Now I want you to take things a step further, practicing creating the space of "Who knows?" We are so busy saying we know, just like my brother and me in the first exercise. We have it figured out. We have the answers. We know what is good and what is bad. We know it all....

But deep down, you and I both know that in truth, sometimes—maybe even most of the time—we don't know shit. We guess, we assume, we project, we predict; we very rarely know. There's no instruction manual that comes with living a human life, and we don't often know what our choices will produce. No one person or group of people have it all figured out. We haven't solved world peace, global hunger, war, or the killing of our neighbors or of strangers. We don't know.

My good friend Nate is a brilliant guy. We joke that he has a hard drive for a brain because he can remember so many things, from how to wire a secondary battery to set up a fridge and microwave in your camper van, to the details of a story you told him about your childhood that even you have forgotten. He can play a million musical instruments and figure out just about anything on a computer. "Not knowing is the most we could ever know," he said to me once. "For me, when I can admit I don't know, I feel smarter."

This caught my interest, so I pressed him further: "Why is that?"

He thought for a moment before simply saying, "I feel more myself—more real."

Something in this struck a deeper chord for me, so I wanted to dive beneath it (which by now you can see is a pattern I enjoy!) and discover what else there was to know about not-knowing. How had moving through not-knowing brought Nate to a feeling of wholeness, of being more truly himself?

The key, I think, is that moving into not-knowing freed him from the ego. Not-knowing creates immense fear for the ego; it feels like it must know because the feeling of certainty is often how we survive. Perhaps we have learned that "knowing" is expected of us, no matter what; and that in order to be accepted and ultimately loved, we must perform this constant certainty. Over time, perhaps we get so used to our imagined certainty that uncertainty becomes a space we can barely tolerate for long. If the universe feels known, measured, and sure, we feel safe. Letting ourselves feel the uncertainty, the unknown, the unpredictable complexity of this place, and our own fragility and vulnerability to it—well, to be frank, that just scares us shitless.

But I have a secret for you: There's an exquisite opening within the I-don't-know. When we can build a tolerance to our own feelings of fear around it and instead practice embracing and sitting with it, the uncertainty creates this moment—this sliver of space and time, like when I quit bickering with my brother, or when Nate said "I don't know"— that stuns the ego. Miraculously, it creates a space there for something more.

Picture a pressure cooker, full to bursting, lid tightly shut. That's what our spirits are like when in the dominating grip of our egos. Nothing can go in; nothing can come out. Nothing moves or changes.

Embracing not knowing is like a release valve on the pressure cooker. It lets the steam escape, breaking the seal, the stasis, and allowing you to finally open the lid and access the nourishing food within. If you can't release the pressure, you can't open the lid and feast. When our ego is taking up all the space with pretending to know everything, there's no room for our heart's compass to learn something new.

So once we make the space, releasing the steam through the I-don't-know, we find the god within. It is a subtle yet powerful form of surrender, and what we find through surrender is the divine. This is the gateway to it. This is the opening that you're looking for, and it will begin to change everything.

We will go into surrender more deeply in the final part of the book. But for now, let's start here. As part of this practice, you can even reuse some of the examples that you came up with in Part One for "Reframing the Whys," if you like. If you feel you've already moved on from those, then go ahead and choose some other examples. (They usually aren't hard to come by!) Write down several experiences you have had; did you assign them as good or bad? Then we will take our next steps.

•••

For this second part, you don't need to write anything down. Instead, I want you to finish writing up your examples and find a quiet place to sit. Maybe you have a meditation spot or an altar; if not, just find a quiet place where you won't be disturbed for a while. Put your phone away, close yourself off from distractions like kids, work, or partners, and just be.

Now pick the first example on your list, read it, and close your eyes. In your head, revisit that example, letting yourself feel how sure you are that it was good or bad. And then, just let yourself loosen your hold on that feeling of certainty. Sit in the

I-don't-know. Start, perhaps, with What if I don't know? Let that idea open up inside of you. Repeat over and over to yourself: I don't know. I don't know. I. Don't. Know.

After a minute or so, I want you to simply stop and listen. Don't talk. Don't process. Just listen. Feel yourself sitting in the space of the I-don't-know, and see what you find there. I'll give you a hint: love will be there. Right there with you. The god within.

PART III

THE
EMERGENCE

CHAPTER FIVE

Approaching Transition

"That night, I knew I would get away, better myself. Not because I despised who I was, but because I did not know who I was. I was waiting to be invented. I was waiting to invent myself."
—JEANETTE WINTERSON

L ife is transition. We are constantly moving, changing, evolving, breathing, creating, being, doing, coming, going, sleeping, waking, growing, maturing, living, and dying. We are in perpetual motion. This very cosmos is constantly in transition: the planets, the stars, the tides, the seasons. There is only becoming.

The fact of the matter is that none of us are ever what we once were, entirely. Even our cells change; 330 billion cells in our bodies are replaced daily! In other words, there's a whole new you on the scene after about 100 days have gone by. We are no longer our teenage selves, or our toddler selves. We have transitioned into a new self. And we do it every day. But humans...we struggle deeply with change. Most of us hate it and fight against it with the ferocity of a mother lioness protecting her cubs. How odd it is, though, to resist what is inevitable.

I resisted change for decades. I *hated* change. I wanted so desperately to hold on to what I knew and was comfortable with... or so I thought. Not until death struck again—so deeply close to home this time, with Creta's passing—did I fully realize that I was following my fear, yet again. Fear was telling me that change was not to be trusted. It told me that others—the ones who mattered, the ones who could wipe me out if they left me—couldn't handle change or grow with me. Fear had me convinced that I'd already left too many things and people behind to make yet another transition in this life. I was terrified to really emerge as my true self (at least in that very moment, since of course I was already changing again and again, even as this process was transpiring).

Yet when Creta died, it became an undeniable wakeup call for me.

The Gerhart family, as I mentioned, had been a second family to me. Alice and I had known each other since high school, and she had been one of the few close friends who actually stuck by me when shit hit the fan. When Anya and I had our faux wedding (as we called it, because queer people couldn't get legally married back then), the only family who showed up for me was my brother, his wife, and one cousin. But the Gerharts were there. When Anya danced with her dad at our reception, Harry Gerhart jumped up from his seat, grabbed my hand, and led me out on that dance floor, both of us in snappy black suits and ties, laughing, connecting, as he became my dad for that moment in time.

And so, when Creta told us near the end of her life that what mattered—*all* that mattered—was loving one another, her words hit me. *Hard.* Death and loss, whether our own or that of people we love, are often times of reckoning, of thinking back on the story of our lives. Creta's words got me thinking. What mattered also was loving myself. I began to look back over the years of work I had done, the struggle, the slow growing, and I could see as though from a bird's-eye view how all of this work had been a journey home to myself—finding a way to love myself as I am, and to fully be myself in the world. I knew it wasn't a one-and-done thing; I had to continue repeating the work, over and over again (and I still do, even to this day). But when Creta died, I could tell. The time, once more, had come, and it meant a process of coming out yet again, but in a whole new way. I knew—somehow, I just knew—I had to take a leap.

I finally feared the idea of staying where I was more than I feared becoming the man I knew I was.

Of course, I have never done things the easy way or taken the straightforward path. (You're likely picking that up by now.) So my transition wasn't just about the physical transition of my body—which I'll share with you—but it was also a process taking place on the emotional and spiritual planes. In essence, my entire life was in transition. I could no longer go on as I was.

We all know the story of how a caterpillar becomes a butterfly. But did you know that the caterpillar is born already containing the cells that will enable it to become a butterfly? The same is true for all of us. Everything we will become already lives within

us, awaiting the right moment. It was time to find the truth of this
for myself.

•••

Telling my story has been challenging to me for many reasons,
but one big challenge is how to convey the process. As the writer
Sue Monk Kidd puts it, "Rarely is any awareness or process on
this journey a one-time event. We seem to return to it over and
over, each time integrating it a bit more fully, owning it a little
more deeply."

**We tell stories in straight lines,
but as we live, we live in cycles.**

Our journeys are like spiral staircases: As we ascend, we return
to what may look like the same view, but we are accessing it
from a new, different perspective. Although in this book I have
separated three parts of my journey into distinct chapters—the
apocalypse, my transition, and my reemergence spiritually—in real
life, these events were taking place nearly simultaneously and in
overlapping ways.

Entering transition, then, was the same: cyclic, and touched by
all the other parts of my life, the other storylines that were taking
place. Between Dorris's early question, "Would you ever want to
go by *he*?," and the time I finally felt comfortable coming out as
trans, going by my true name, and using "he/him" pronouns, years
(and the apocalypse) had gone by. Creta had died, and I had
begun rebuilding my relationship with the god within. It would take
another year after that before I could get top surgery (a double

mastectomy to remove all breast tissue), and still another six to eight months before I could change my legal name and update all the endless paperwork of modern life.

Just as Creta was diagnosed, the transition process had begun—at least in my own mind. I started talking to my therapist about the idea, about maybe risking going by *he* and floating the thought of at least getting a breast reduction. That thought felt amazing to me, although even then I could tell it was less than what I truly desired (but couldn't *possibly* say out loud).

But this therapist and I were definitely not on the same page. Even as I began talking about how interested I was in the possibility of transitioning—how I had always known myself to be a boy, but had never had the space to allow myself the courage to claim that, until these very moments—the therapist was not at all open. She immediately began to push back on the idea of even a breast reduction and seemed totally against even discussing the true thing I desired: a double mastectomy. Something in that moment awakened an energy in me. In the past, I might have acquiesced and simply stifled my desires, but I could no longer do so. As we started to clash, I realized that that professional relationship was not a space to explore more deeply who I was and where I wanted my life to go.

That was when I remembered a friend's recommendation, a while back, of a different therapist. "You should try her," my friend had advised. "She actually specializes in therapy for trans people." At the time, I was stunned. I was so surprised that a therapist like that could even exist, let alone in fucking *Texas*. I wasn't sure I was ready then, but I stored it away in my mind, knowing I would come back to it at some point.

Sure enough, when my first therapist and I began clashing, the memory resurfaced—and helped me get up the courage to leave the therapist I was seeing at the time and consider working with a new one. That initial therapeutic relationship had been a useful tool at the beginning; the sessions certainly helped me stop my debilitating panic attacks. But then their usefulness dried up—and led me right out the door to the next step of my journey.

On the way out of my old therapist's office, I passed an acupuncture practice, which I had already walked by every week for several months. That day, something pulled me inside, and I made one appointment that turned into many.

I'll be honest. Those sessions were hard work. My acupuncturist would arrange the needles, then leave me "to relax for a while." Within 10 minutes, I'd want to scream her name until she came and released me from the massive emotions arising in me. Session after session, it became clear: *That's* what I was running from.

I was running from being alone with myself.

I was mostly fine when I was with other people. I could always put on a good show, turn on my charisma and my extrovert self, and have everyone laughing and yukking it up in moments. But alone? What a nightmare. As I experienced that terror of aloneness in the acupuncturist's office, I began to understand how old this fear was. Even my six-year-old self had had it. Every night, when his parents had left him tucked in bed, he scurried out and down the hallway to find out what everyone else was up to, sneaking around the back of the couch to sit quietly, relieved just to not be alone.

Recognizing this through line of fear in my life was astonishing to me.

> **I was reacting to being alone with myself as though aloneness was death. Because if I'm separate from god—which I feared I was—then if I am alone, I am cut off from all life, warmth, connection, meaning, joy, and growth.**

The ultimate separation, the ultimate death. *This* is what I had been running from. This is why I kept wanting to move around, make new friends, or have something to do. I couldn't sit still and just be within myself, because alone, I would surely die.

No wonder losing things, communities, and people had become so hard for me. I had no calm center of connection to the god within that would allow me to realize when tools became less tool and more shovel-in-a-well. The god within would have helped this feel normal. *It's time to move on from this,* the quiet voice would have said, and I could have done so trusting that new connections, new tools, would appear. No wonder I was deep in that well, frantically clutching my shovel, terrified of laying it down. Without that connection to the god within, all I knew was that anything that was ever taken from me was the worst possible thing ever; everyone I lost made me relive feeling abandoned by my family—and my god.

Does any of this resonate with you and your experience? Does your life contain some through lines of your own fears and deep pain? Perhaps you, too, have suffered from the fear that you are alone in this world, having to fend for yourself, wondering where the universe is and when it will be your turn to be rescued.

At that moment, I had no idea how to get out of the grip of my fear. Maybe you don't, either. *That's okay.* We all get to be at a loss, at the end of our rope, sometimes. We don't even always need to know *what* we need to do in order to save ourselves from our pain. Eventually, a question forms within: How do we move—even just a bit—through a stuck place? How can we face the stuckness, when facing it feels like dying?

But as the days passed for me, and the pressures, losses, and pain grew more undeniable, I realized: *If I don't face all this stuff, surely I'm going to die anyway.*

•••

It's the spring of 2015, just a week after Creta's death. After a nice memorial service for her, we've all returned to the family house to eat food and be together. Creta's kitchen has this amazing step stool because the cabinets are extremely tall, and Alice—who is shorter than me by more than a foot—jumps up on the step stool and wraps her arms around my neck. We stand there hugging and crying over her mom.

Suddenly I feel a sensation, like a gust of wind. It rushes into the house and blows across my face. Looking around, I can see that no one else notices or feels it. All the doors and windows are closed. And without being able to explain how I know this, I *know*: The wind is carrying a message for me, from Creta—about Dorris. It's Dorris who is rushing in through the air.

Dorris and Alice are the same height. And Dorris used to climb up on a step stool, one I got from my grandmother, and hug me—just as Alice has just done, except Alice has never done it before. With her arms around my neck like that, I am stunned to feel Dorris.

She and I haven't spoken in nine months, and I have so often wished to speak to her, especially when Creta's journey with cancer has reminded me of her own a few years earlier. Dorris had been diagnosed with leukemia, and I feared losing her to cancer. Her unexpected remission meant that I didn't—and then I still lost her (friendship) anyway. What a mess.

I drive home from the Gerharts' sobbing, feeling Alice's arms around me and Dorris somehow in that embrace. Soon I'm wiping the tears streaming down my face as if I'm a windshield wiper in a Texas rainstorm. As I drive, a voice is speaking from deep inside of me: the quiet, subtle voice of my god within. It whispers, *Call Dorris....* I don't know what the voice is thinking! But I hear it again. *Call Dorris.*

"I'm *not* calling her," I shout into the silence of my car.

When I get home, I go to bed, only to wake in the morning with the same gnawing feeling inside me, and the same voice whispering, *Call Dorris....* This is unbelievable! "I am. *Not. Calling. Her,*" I yell at the universe, at my guides, at god—whatever the hell it is that keeps making this terrible suggestion. Louder this time, so it will get the message. There is *no way* I am calling her. She's hurt and abandoned me, hasn't she? My wounded pride flares up at this thought, and I begin stomping around the house, making coffee and arguing with god.

I spend the next couple of hours in a wrestling match with god, which I lose. Within a few minutes, my phone is in my hand, and my traitorous fingers are calling Dorris's number. It's like something in me, some hidden bravery of trusting myself just enough, has begun to push me into transition—toward the person I know I can be.

The phone rings. And rings. And goes to voicemail. *What on Earth do I say?* I hang up, feeling awkward.

I text Anya for quick advice. *What should I do? What if Dorris thinks it was only a butt dial?* "

Just text her, then," Anya writes back.

Right. Logic. Okay. So I send Dorris a quick text telling her the call wasn't accidental; I am wondering if we can talk. She writes back, very surprised; she *had* assumed it was an accident. Today doesn't work to talk; what about tomorrow?

I not-so-patiently wait. The next morning, after a few hundred years have gone by, the phone rings. *Her.* Her voice sounds like light streaming through a beautiful stained glass window. So familiar, yet so new and fresh. We talk and talk and talk, for three hours, about Creta's passing, about her grandmother's death, about how much we've missed one another—and how sorry we both are. We both apologize more in those three hours than we have in the previous 10 years of friendship.

I can barely take in what is happening. Is this real? Is the universe really bringing her back to me?

Six weeks later, I board a plane to Arizona to visit her. I land in Phoenix late at night, rent a car, and begin the two-and-half-hour drive north to Flagstaff—a deeply ironic drive, as some 19 years earlier, I drove into this town and arrived at my college dorm room: the same one where I met and dated Aviva in secret, and where I told my friend Samantha that her dad was going to hell for being gay. The same small town, and this is now where my Dorris lives. What are the chances?

The two-and-a-half-hour drive that night feels like it takes 10 years. As soon as I see the sign "Welcome to Flagstaff," I begin to cry. I finally pull onto her street, and there she is, waiting outside for me on a cool June night. I park the car and quickly get out. She leaps into my arms, wrapping her legs around my waist and her arms around my neck, hugging me fiercely there on the street at nearly midnight. Her energy in that moment is exactly the wind that rushed into Creta's house that night of her funeral, as Alice and I stood hugging on a step stool.

And I know that, in some mystical way, it's Creta who brought me back to Dorris.

●●●

If anyone had seen me in those moments of stomping around my house, yelling at my guides for telling me to call Dorris, they probably would have thought I had completely lost it. But looking back from where I stand now, I can see how amazing those moments actually were. I was in dialogue with god again. Sure, I was yelling—but we were talking. We were in communion.

Something was changing within me, even if I didn't know it yet.

While the time apart from my friendship with Dorris—a full nine months, which we noted later as a definite nod from the universe to something new that needed to be birthed—had been massively difficult, it was also true that I had taken that time to do some serious work with myself.

Originally, my connection with Dorris had brought me back to the god within; or, at the very least, it had made an opening where I'd thought I knew for sure that a door would never open again. Suddenly, right in that space of deadness and pain, this miraculous friend had begun helping me reconnect with the thing that had left the biggest void in my life.

No surprise, then, that earlier in our friendship I had begun to attach Dorris to god. I think of it this way: Mainstream Protestant Christianity uses Jesus to get to god; Catholics pray to Mary as an intercessor on their behalf. For me, it was as though I began to use Dorris as an intercessory to my connection with the divine. When we had done things together like meditation, or simply talking about the last spiritual book we read, it had felt amplified, somehow larger or more powerful than if I had just done it on my own.

But that's a lot of pressure for one person—to be the bat-phone to god for you. It's no wonder that our relationship came crashing down. It *had* to. I had to learn to do the work on my own, to find my own connection to the god within me, and to truly find myself underneath all of the debris that had crumbled down onto me.

So by the time I arrived in Flagstaff that night in June, I felt like I was a different version of myself. More confident. Less needy. I had begun to build up my own relationship with the divine, from the ground up this time; I didn't need a conduit in the form of Dorris anymore. She was free to just be Dorris. And she recognized that shift in my energy almost immediately.

Dorris and I and some other friends spent a few days together at her house. By the third day, everyone else had left, and it was just the two of us. In our friendship up until then, we had always been in a limbo space: completely in sync at times, and then utterly and completely out of sync in almost the next breath. Yet now it was apparent that what had shifted for both of us during that nine-month hiatus had opened up space for this...this *possibility*. We were both in relationships that were "open," meaning we each had agreements with our partners to see other people too.

The first night she and I spent alone in Flagstaff, while watching a movie, something lit on fire between our energies, and we kissed. And not just any kiss; it was a kiss that I honestly believe sent sparks of light and fireworks rippling throughout all space and time. In that kiss, I could feel more than just 10 years of pent-up attraction and love for one another; I could feel thousands of years.

And here we come to one of those points I talked about at the beginning of the chapter: a place where one storyline blurs with and affects another. During my spiritual journey, which I will talk more about in the next chapter, I had, through meditation and shamanic work, accessed visions of past lifetimes. These lifetimes I had come across resonated with me deeply. They felt so familiar, and some of them were lifetimes in which I had known and loved Dorris. When she kissed me in this life, it was as though all the worlds collided, and the line between past lives and this one blurred spectacularly. I knew more than ever that we had been destined to find each other again and to love one another in this lifetime as well. Somehow, unbelievably, I knew—I knew, more truly than anything I have ever known, and certainly more than I can possibly explain: It was her. I was him. This was us. And it was meant to happen at this time and in this way.

But when we think we've reached one destination, another journey begins, right?

•••

While Dorris and I changed our internal worlds in that very instant, the outside world wasn't exactly going to change as quickly. But watch out, world, because the Born a Day Early guy was on the scene again, and this time I wasn't running from something; I was running *toward* it. Toward my truest self. Everything seemed to be happening simultaneously, and also, paradoxically, nothing seemed to be happening. Maybe that's how the caterpillar feels while it's both digesting itself and also in a state of frozenness within the chrysalis. For a while, I went around and around about what name I wanted to go by. Finally I settled on Alex, a name with familial significance, and he (him, his, etc.) as my pronoun. And so began the journey of telling people and coming out.

I retrieved the phone number of the therapist my friend had recommended, the one who specialized in work with trans patients, and made my first appointment. The time had come. For the first time in therapy, I felt truly safe to be my authentic self and to engage deeply with the issues I had around my gender. Not only did we work through things using a traditional therapeutic model; we also used shamanic journey work. It was a perfect pairing for me: my spirituality and shamanic experience, on the one hand, and the need to have a traditional therapist who was able to write me the letter I needed for surgery, on the other.

A few words about surgery. People don't always realize this, but even as an adult almost 40 years old at the time, I couldn't just make the decision to have top surgery and then find a doctor. Before going to a doctor, I had to see a therapist for at least six months, and that therapist had to be willing to write me a letter attesting to that, giving their professional opinion on the appropriateness of my surgery, and confirming that I'd been living life as a man for at least six months: using he/him pronouns, going by Alex, and so on. There were all these rules to be met just so I could be me.

A new year came and went, and we reached 2016. This was it; this was the year! I finally got on the schedule with the surgeon's office, and I was set to have my surgery in October. In and of itself, that seemed like a million years away. But still, there was more work to be done. I continued with my therapy, which was important, since things began to both unravel and evolve all at once.

For one thing, it became clear for me and Anya, my partner of 16 years, that our relationship had come to an end. We were simply no longer the people we had been to each other. In a lot of ways, we had both known that for a while, but things had been so comfortable and truly easy between us that it was hard to let that go.

Now, mind you, sometimes relationships do break up when one of the people within them transitions—but it usually happens, as it did for us, because it's a time of movement and reevaluation that can often lead to change. Anya had always been undyingly supportive of who I became, no matter what that looked like, and in fact, even though it ended up happening months after our breakup, she was there with me at my surgery, together with both Alice and Dorris. During this period, Dorris also broke up with her partner. It had become evident to us both that we could no longer deny the way we felt about each other, and we were pulled toward seeing where our relationship could go if we both stepped fully and completely into it, without any other people involved.

So life was about to look very different. Anya had walked with me through some of the very hardest times of my life: through my coming out, and the destruction left in its wake; through a decade and a half of depression, anxiety, and addiction; and also through amazing joy, fun, excitement, and sheer *life*. She was an incredible, supportive partner and someone I will treasure in my heart forever. I couldn't have made it through all those years without her; I wouldn't be here today, in fact. So letting go of our marriage was difficult, even though it was the right thing for us both.

● ● ●

As the date for the surgery approached, I began to notice a new, sometimes unsettling energy rise up in me. For so long, I had lived in familiar fear and despair. But now that was changing. I was starting to long to be...hopeful.

Hope is the fertile soil from which a fulfilled life grows. Hope leads to a thriving space for growth and change, for evolution and expansion. Hope breeds life, laying the foundation for trust and faith in both the process and the outcome.

That kind of energy was not one I had lived with, not for a very long time. I was accustomed to hope's opposite: despair. Despair, more often than not, leads to perceived failures—meaning that, when things don't even remotely turn out how we would have liked them to, we decide the whole experience was a failure. In the grip of despair, we believe in our failure diagnosis so completely that there is no room for any new insight or perspective. We are in such pain, and so angry about the reality of outcomes we didn't want, that we spend most of our energy looking for ways to blame others for our pain in this world.

An enormous part of our human discomfort is our wavering back and forth between these two energies: hope and despair. Like a seesaw, back and forth, left and right—hope rides high, then despair overtakes it. Hope, despair; hope, despair.

My last few years had been filled with despair, and with the fears it leads to. I was up to my neck in anger and pain, frantically trying to blame everyone else for how badly I was hurting. I had been blaming my family, society, the church—heck, the poor driver with the fish bumper sticker on their car: blame, blame, blame. Pointing my finger at all the people, from my parents to Dorris to god, who had betrayed, abandoned, neglected, or traumatized me, whose love had been seemingly rescinded, causing—as I saw it—the hell that my very existence had become. I kept lashing out, furious at these things and people that seemed to be responsible for my hurt. As my transition took its next turn, I came face-to-face with this profound truth, which would be the hardest I had yet encountered:

NO ONE ELSE WAS RESPONSIBLE FOR MY PAIN.

If anyone had tried to tell me that even a year earlier, I probably would have bitten their head off. It was so much easier—or at least, so I thought—to ride high on despair's side of the seesaw, proclaiming that *that* person, *those* people, society, and whoever else were the reason for my discomfort. I was prepared to yell it from the rooftops for the rest of my miserable days, if I had to.

I didn't know it at the time—because deep in despair, I felt completely alone—but it turns out I was walking a path countless others had walked before me, a human drama as old as humanity itself. Blame leads to victimhood, and victimhood leads to a vicious cycle that is incredibly hard to end. All wars, all human rights atrocities, all murder and hatred stem from victimhood and the idea of blaming someone else for our despair. Most "isms" and phobias are rooted in this pattern. With racism, "those people" are the reason for high crime rates, unemployment, or the degradation of society. Homophobia and transphobia show up in language tossed around like "Trans women aren't 'real' women," or the idea that a nefarious gay agenda is at work to brainwash kids (and adults too) and unravel the fabric of a "godly society." We always look for someone else to blame for the issues we are facing in our lives, our generation, and our world, and it's never pretty when this happens. Go ahead: Try and think of an instance of injustice from history or from stories that isn't us trying to blame our way out from under our pain by scapegoating someone, or even whole groups of people. I'll wait.

Nothing, right? You can't come up with one, because that's how this works. And this is part of our collective work through to the other side: our work of transition. We have a high, beautiful calling here. We must find the consciousness in ourselves to see when we are on the despair side of the seesaw, and rather than setting up home base there, to instead shift our weight, so to speak; to keep moving, to give hope its turn to rise.

Of course, at times this is very difficult work. Do you remember when you were a kid, if you got on the seesaw with someone roughly your size, the seesaw felt evenly balanced? Sometimes you were up, then you would go down, and the person on the other side would rise. But did you ever end up out of balance—with a bigger, older kid on the other side, or maybe with a smaller kid too light to balance your weight? Can you drop into your body's memory of how it felt when it became really hard to move up and down—how eventually, your small self was just stuck? When despair becomes a habit, this is exactly the way the problem feels. We lose the fluidity, the motion, the ability to change perspectives that comes from rising and falling in turn. We're stuck high up in the air, no way to get down; or we're stuck on the ground, no way to rise.

Our work is to find more balance. We will all feel despair sometimes; it's a normal human emotion, and none of us will ever arrive at a place in life where we simply don't have to feel the particular emotions we don't like. Instead, we get better at *working* with those emotions. The emotions hijack us less. We find ways to be less triggered, which allows us to stay closer to our true selves even when the hard emotions show up. With this practice, we can actually lessen or lighten despair. Yes, sometimes despair is riding high on our seesaw, but we don't have to stay in that state and let ourselves shift into a state of blame; that's where problems get created. Instead, we allow for the despair to pass and the hope to return.

This starts small, and the going can be very slow at first. It certainly was for me. In the early stages of transition, even wanting to be hopeful felt scary to me, sometimes. But I began simple acts of affirming hope: hope that next time, things can be different; hope that next time I will respond differently, or that my loved one will too. Hope that tomorrow will be a new day in which I can make a full effort to be my best self—not in spite of the adversity in my life, but because no matter what is going on around me, I can be true to myself and access my highest good.

I won't bullshit you. This change wasn't easy, quick, or exciting. But it *was* where I began to find more relief. Sitting constantly in the place of despair, looking for someone and something to blame for my experiences in life, had only led to more despair and suffering. Seeking out hope and learning to access faith through it, over time, started to shift everything. And in the process of shifting from my habits of blame and despair, I soon came up against my inner saboteur: the hidden part of myself that had been making mischief in every situation and relationship of my life, but that I had been totally unable to see as long as I was focused on projecting blame outward.

We all have an inner saboteur in our personalities, as part of our ego. This is the part of us that seemingly deliberately disrupts us, delays us, and hinders us from progress or growth. Our inner saboteur may even, in some ways, try to destroy us. Oftentimes its behavior comes out of a desire the ego has to protect us, thinking it's safer to stay how we are and who we are, because if we change or grow, we might not need the ego anymore. It thinks its acts are self-preservation, but in fact, they often detract from our experience. For example, we might be drawn to an idea: "Oh, I'd really love to sit down, read this book, and relax for a half hour. That would improve my whole day, and I know I can make time for it." Our inner saboteur might counter that: "You don't have time to sit and relax! You have a million things left to do on your to-do list. Get up and get going, or you'll never get it done." The first idea felt great and would have taken us downstream—meaning, we would be going *with* the flow, following something that sounded enjoyable and felt *right*—but we don't do it because we talk ourselves out of it. That's the inner saboteur in us all.

And this is the kicker: when we're deep in victim mentality, aware only of the ways people and things "out there" are making us suffer, we can't see that inner saboteur at work, making us suffer far more constantly than anything out in the world possibly could. Mine was on the job full time: with me everywhere I went, and keeping me in familiar habits of fear and despair in all the spaces of my life.

This is a law of the universe: We reap what we sow. When we sow more hope, the crops we reap will be manifestations of that hope.

As we sow more hope and more beauty in our life, colors will be brighter; life will feel smoother and more fulfilled. Access to our highest good and our divine direction will come much more easily.

And then, when the despair hits again and the hard stuff rises—which it will—we will have a wider frame of reference for the hope and the benefits of returning to that state, and we won't stay as long in the despair.

This was what I began to see as I transitioned from a life dominated by despair and fear, to a life lived with hope and faith. I'd been holding on to this idea that I was a victim in all the circumstances in my life—that everyone had done all this damage to me, and that ultimately they had tried to destroy me, because somehow I wasn't good enough or valued enough even to be allowed to survive. But slowly, a new understanding emerged. I wasn't a victim; I was *victimized*. Dr. Edith Eva Eger speaks of this beautifully in her book *The Choice*:

> *My own search for freedom and my years of experience as a licensed clinical psychologist have taught me that suffering is universal. But victimhood is optional. There is a difference between victimization and victimhood. We are all likely to be victimized in some way in the course of our lives. At some point we will suffer some kind of affliction or calamity or abuse, caused by circumstances or people or institutions over which we have little or no control. This is life. And this is victimization. It comes from the outside. It's the neighborhood bully, the boss who rages, the spouse who hits, the lover who cheats, the discriminatory law, the accident that lands you in the hospital.*

In contrast, victimhood comes from the inside. No one can make you a victim but you. We become victims not because of what happens to us but when we choose to hold on to our victimization. We develop a victim's mind—a way of thinking and being that is rigid, blaming, pessimistic, stuck in the past, unforgiving, punitive, and without healthy limits or boundaries. We become our own jailers when we choose the confines of the victim's mind.

Shifting that language began to open up a new pathway for me.

If I wasn't The Victim, but instead I was just victimized, that meant I had options. I could move around; there was space and agency for me. A victim is helpless, at the mercy of others, of cruel fate, and most especially, of that inner saboteur. But someone who was victimized? They're not helpless; they're human. And being human means they can tell a new story, grow, adapt, get unstuck, and release their grip on old pains.

That let me shift out of blame and see each perpetrator as someone who had their own pain, trauma, and fear that they were working out, just as I was with mine. However they had acted toward me, their choices and reactions were about them playing out their own issues, and less about me. Chances were, they too were struggling under the merciless reign of their own inner saboteur. Any part of their reaction that was about me was a learning opportunity that was coming up for me to heal. That felt different to me energetically, and again things began to shift more deeply in me. Healing was making its way through my soul and heart.

There is a moment always available to us, a moment of turning that is never too late for us to take. As I said, we are constantly moving and evolving; we are in perpetual motion. My moment had come.

Maybe this is yours.

At this moment of transition in my story, I want to pause and invite you to enter yours. Find the ground again, then push your feet off from it; rise up from the side of hope once more. See the sun on the horizon, take some fresh perspective, and see what you can grow from here.

Maybe it's time to let that inner saboteur go, and to recognize: there is only becoming.

Dear beloved, inner saboteur self, this is what I want to tell you...

Good work, inner saboteur. You've done the ego's bidding for so long now, and so well. We thank you for your service and relieve you of duty. There isn't work for you going forward; you are outdated and underappreciated around here. It's time you go somewhere else—somewhere you can rest, knowing you will be held. The sweet spirit reading these words right now is ready for a new part of the journey; you have misdirected them long enough.

But we know you were just doing your job. It's not your fault; you simply did what the ego told you. That's all it knows. But the soul knows better, and it's time to let it be the guiding light over this one's ego and their inner saboteur. So today, as they mark yet another revolution around the Earth's sun, we help them plant their foot solidly on the ground and take new steps toward their new future.

Dear, struggling self, you have spent your 40 years in the desert wandering, looking for nourishment from god, building your false idols, finding your truth path, and now you're ready to go forward. You are ready to move on from that time, that experience, of searching and waiting, longing and aching for something to fill your soul. You know now what fills your soul; you have found what fills your soul. It may not be complete yet, but you can tell from these first tastes what it feels like to be filled with abundance and grace, knowledge and wisdom, love and light, gratitude and compassion. Those first tastes are enough to tell you which direction to go, toward the space where you can live more fully from your heart space, and less from your ego.

And that, beloved, is what you have been searching for all these lifetimes and longing for so deeply in this life—so much so that you could have at times just burst at your seams. You have felt this way because you are made of light. You are one with the light; there is no light that is not within you or is without you. You are the very source of the light and meant to be a beacon of it. There are no mistakes or missed opportunities. Everything will return in its own cycle for revisiting again.

I implore you, then, in this moment, to stand before me, your beloved, and make this commitment to yourself—to us. You are worth this, and believe me when I say, it's crucial. So pack up your rucksack, grab that walking stick, and let's head into the promised land. Be willing—you certainly are able—to walk into this uncharted territory, as unfamiliar as it may seem. I promise you it is time.

Dear Beloved writing prompt

Ask the god within, who knows you when you get stuck on the wrong end of despair, to guide you: Where do I notice my inner saboteur, claiming that I am The Victim, preventing me from seeing my own agency and ability for change? How do I encourage the saboteur to pack its bags, to relinquish control to you?

Write down what the god within has to say: "Dear beloved...."

CHAPTER SIX

ENTERING TRANSITION

*"Transformation is a journey
without a final destination."*
—MARILYN FERGUSON

Welcome, friend. Welcome to the other side, as together we all practice transitioning, renewing connection to our higher selves. As you and I will discover—as all of us who traverse this path discover—this is a process, not a one-time event. But we take the journey side by side.

As I got closer to my surgery, and the physical transition this event would mark for me, fear kept trying to overtake faith. I admitted to myself and Dorris that part of me was very scared to go under the knife. Would I wake up? Would it all be okay? I didn't know. But what I did know was that I wanted a chance to live in this world as my true, authentic self, and in order to do this—for me—I needed to get the surgery.

●●●

It's the night before my surgery. Dorris and I lie in bed in a hotel room just a few miles from the surgery center. We talk most of the night, resting in each other's arms and savoring these moments in case something goes wrong in surgery and they are our last. What a trip.

The morning comes.

We arrive in the waiting room. Within a few minutes, Anya and Alice find their way in, carrying coffee for everyone, excitedly hugging us. We all sit down to wait. A few minutes pass, and then a nurse comes through the door. "Alex Reegan?"

I nod and raise my hand, finally managing to croak out, "That's me."

"You can all come back now," the nurse says, smiling encouragingly.

We wander through the doors in the surgical center's cold, sterile hallway and enter a room with several chairs and a hospital bed. They tell me to change out of my clothes into a gown they've given me. A bit later, the doctor comes in, an enormous smile on his face, and I marvel again that somehow, in the middle of Texas, I have found a very trans-affirming expert in the field of trans surgeries who is excited to accompany and help me on this part of my journey.

At last, I say my goodbyes to Dorris, Anya, and Alice—three people who somehow represent my past, present, and future. Then they wheel me into the OR...across the threshold, and into transition.

●●●

The next thing I'm aware of is Dorris telling me to take a drink of something cold and bubbly. I try to use the straw, but I feel so groggy. I open my eyes and look down. My whole chest is wrapped in giant bandages, and instead of just the loose hospital gown, I am wearing shorts. I look at Dorris, and I look at my shorts. It feels incredibly confusing. I'm trying to form this important question, but my brain is sluggish. Finally I manage to speak: "How did I get pants on?"

"We all helped you," she says, smiling at me. I have *no* recollection of that. It's as though, in transition, I have entered a second infancy—unable even to dress myself, needing others to help me.

Within a half hour, the hospital staff shuttle me to our car, and we head back to the hotel, where our bestie Nate has arrived to help Dorris care for me over the next few days. Top surgery is an outpatient procedure, and apart from a nurse hotline, you are on your own for the complex and often grueling recovery. Reading through the discharge paperwork, we come upon a large note that said, "DO NOT MAKE ANY BIG DECISIONS OVER THE NEXT FEW DAYS."

I stare at the note. Then I start grinning. "Like I'm gonna phone the doctor and say, 'Hey doc, now when can I get a dick?' You think that's the kind of big decisions they're talking about?"

We all burst out laughing, and for several moments, loopy yet thrilled to be sitting in a hotel room with my favorite people all in one place, I completely forget the pain that has brought me there.

●●●

The days after that felt surreal. I would look down at myself and finally see a flat chest where size 44DD breasts used to invade. For so long, I had felt as though I was trapped in the wrong body. Now, when I looked at myself, I *recognized* him. It was miraculous. I never in my wildest dreams had thought I could have this.

●●●

Dorris let my parents know that I went into surgery and came out okay. They received the information, but there was no talking or discussions about it, nor have there been any since then. The transition, for them, has not been an easy one. My mom still often cries over the name she gave me at birth, because she named me after a person who was important to her. They struggle to use my real name and pronouns as well. Dorris and I have asked them just to try saying "A," "honey," or "kiddo"—anything easier for them that is not disrespectful and erasing of me—but to no avail, unfortunately.

In the end, though, my way forward was becoming clear: No matter what other people chose for themselves, and no matter the pushback I might face from family, community, or society, I would keep going on my own path, being myself, calmly and without apology. My energies did not need to be spent trying to convince or change other people anymore. No, my energies would go toward my own growth and engagement in my life.

The same is likely true for your experience. Though our lives might look different on the outside, I guarantee you the same principles reside within. In the end, we have to trust our own guidance and follow the path that we were meant to follow in this lifetime. We get sidetracked easily by all the other people in our lives directing traffic, but it's ultimately our choice to say "Enough!"—and to step forward in our own knowing.

● ● ●

Two months after surgery, and I was still feeling pretty uncomfortable. When the doctors had prepped us in the months before surgery, they'd said most people felt better after four to six weeks, even returning to work at that point. But I just wasn't recovering. I was so tired, in a lot of pain, and experiencing constant, overall discomfort in my body. Many of those things had been my consistent experience for a lot of my life, but the added physical pain around my incisions was certainly new.

The surgeon had to cut through some major nerve endings, so scars were forming as the body healed. Over time, the nerve endings attempt to reconnect themselves, and you feel these sharp zings and spasms as they are working. It's fascinating how the body rebuilds itself—but also painful.

Our spirits transition and grow in the same way: rebuilding, changing, relearning, reconnecting what was severed, and working with the pain that comes.

We all share in this experience, no matter our backgrounds or identities. This is what it means to be human—to be alive.

● ● ●

If my story were a fairy tale, this would probably be the point where you'd expect us all to live happily ever after. After all, I had finally "arrived," right? From a lifetime of looking down at my physical self and feeling such shame and disgust over this body that just didn't make sense to me, I had at last landed in a body that felt like *me*. The giant boobs that had (literally) stood out like sore thumbs, that were always in my way—in sports, in my personal life, in relationships—were finally gone.

But something interesting happened after they were removed. I kept looking down; now that they were gone, I could see past them for the first time since childhood. And what I saw? I disliked it just as much. Now I could see my stomach—and all the ways I didn't think it was "just right." The extra weight I thought shouldn't be there, and the stretch marks from all the times I had gained large amounts of weight only to somehow lose it again and then gain it right back.

By far, top surgery was one of the best choices I ever made for my mental health as a trans man. But there was another truth to face, too. *If you need to,* the god within whispered to me, *you will always find something to judge.* If we don't actually pay attention to the root, to the core beliefs from which we are operating, then even when we appear to have "fixed" something in our external world that we think will make us feel better, it's unlikely to give us the full peace, the peace of god, that we are looking for.

And what is the peace that I am ultimately looking for? That we are all looking for?

That I'm good enough. That I'm worthy. That this body isn't all that I am, but it's a valuable teaching instrument. That I'm connected. That I am truly not separate from anything or anyone, let alone god.

But these bodies—the way each one looks different, acts differently, responds differently to every stimulus—they make us feel like we are truly separate and different from each other; they constantly create this illusion of separateness. And we do have to live in this world; we came here to be humans, in this time, in this place. So we do need to attend to our bodies in their separateness; to learn what they need and treat them well; to care for our mental health through caring for our bodies, as I did through my surgery (and perhaps through sobriety earlier too).

But the work in my internal world would be just as important, just as necessary. I had reunited more fully with my body; I had begun the renewal of my connection to my higher self. Now it would be time for me to reunite more deeply with my spirit: with the god within.

Dear beloved, ever-changing self, this is what I want to tell you...

It won't always feel this way, but...

Change is your strong suit; growth is your friend.

The stagnancy—not the becoming—is actually the thing that drives you wild. The becoming is your deepest desire; it is, in fact, what you came here to do. You knew, from before you were born into this world, that this is what this life would hold; you saw the entire picture of the life you would have. You knew exactly what you were stepping into; the only reason it seems like a "surprise" is because that's how being human works. It would be a terrible experience if you humans, from the very beginning, remembered exactly who you were. If you knew all the secrets and the outcomes, what a boring life you would live. Think for a moment of a game you play or a sporting event you watch: if you knew every play, every choice made ahead of time, what boredom you would find! Instead, you essentially come into this life with a memory wipe; although some people still have little bits of information saved to their hard drive, most of you enter as "clean slates." Then the experience unfolds, and many of you begin to remember bits and pieces—some of you more than others—and the experience keeps unfolding, and you grow.

All the while, you are growing into the you that you not only can be, but already are. That's the crux of the game: You were part of the very creation of this place, of this experience; you knew exactly what you were doing creating this, and then dropping your soul into this body and experience. It's never been about punishment or building on your fear; those are unfortunate side effects to human nature, to the ego. But the ego is only in charge if you allow it to be. It doesn't have the authority to do anything unless you sign your powers over to it.

So take time, each day, to remember this situation in a new way, and look at it from this higher perspective. Trust your higher self, knowing that while the smaller you doesn't have all the information about the game, the larger you is the game-maker. That trust, and choosing love over the fear, will keep your experience flowing and in better alignment with who you are at the core of your being.

Think of it like New Year's Day, the idea of starting again, breathing anew—creating new space to set intentions for the coming year. Allow this day to be a setting where you see yourself born again. (HA!) We know that can be a triggering word for some people, but let's rebrand it, reclaim it. Today you are born again, into a new day; a new experience awaits. You can release and allow the past to simply fall away and be that—the past. You need not carry it forward with you in a way that weighs you down. Let the past simply be a guidepost, a reminder of where you came from, knowing that it led you to where you are now. All the bumps, potholes, and detours along this path have been intended. Let go of the notion that you did things wrong or got to where you are in the wrong way. Sometimes you might have taken the scenic route (or, as you all say, the hard way), while others might take the business loop through town and quickly get to that next spot along their map.

The important thing to remember is: There isn't an end point destination that you are trying to get to. The way your society works, it trains you to think about completion, culmination: get through and out of school, go to college and graduate, get married, have a kid, work for 35 years and retire, like one end point after another. But they are all just stops along the way, just as a train reaches a destination and then continues down the track. Sometimes you might take a break, go into the train yard, and be serviced—or in other words, pass on from this life—but then you just get put back out on the tracks and make your way to your next new adventure.

> **If you can find ways to let go of the idea that you need to reach a destination, place of completion, or something that makes it all worthwhile and "done," you will find some of the greatest relief that you are seeking.**

So today, we urge you to sit with this idea. Take in the truth that all of the perceived time that has passed up until now, all the events of your life, have been stops along your journey, and that this is a new part of the same journey. If you all as humans could make this shift, it would make your lives a lot easier. Let this be an awareness that grows in you, and learn to allow it to become something that you pass along as a rule of thumb to those you meet. The bottom line is, it's not only at the start of a year or new chapter that you are born again; it's every single day. That is one of the greatest gifts of knowledge and understanding that you can realize for yourself and share with others. Begin again until it feels like second nature, like a reflex; tremendous expansion will come from this experience, and a rapid advancement toward your next life lesson, which will cut through some of the pain and bullshit that you humans tend to experience so frequently.

So, Happy New Year.... Happy New You.... Try and enjoy the ride.

Dear Beloved writing prompt

Connect with the god within and ask for guidance in these questions: Where have I felt scared off by change, or clung to the desire to hold on to the way things are? How might I be more open and trusting of the universe, knowing that I don't know the train stations ahead, but that my scenic route is you guiding me on my way?

Write the answer: "Dear beloved...."

CHAPTER SEVEN

GOING WITHIN

*"Remember, the entrance door to
the sanctuary is inside you."*
—RUMI

Before we engage with the content of this chapter, a word of clarification. Most of the book up until now has followed a chronological progression; however, as we discussed in Chapter Five, our lives happen cyclically, not linearly. This chapter, even more than the previous ones, will take us out of order; many of the events in it happened during, or even before, the apocalypse and my transition. Bear with me as we travel through time and space in a bit of an unorthodox fashion.

Spiritual growth—just like healing, transformation, and relearning the process of going within—is not a linear event that only happens to us once. It is ongoing, and it ebbs and flows throughout our chronological lives.

In a way, it is fitting that the chapter on going within is the one that most leaves neat chronology behind, because as you will no doubt find for yourself, learning how to go within takes us furthest from external things—and deepest into uncharted and powerful territory. For most of us, we only venture here when we've exhausted all our other options.

There are times in life when it seems that we have surely tried everything, to no avail. We have looked everywhere we can think of outside of ourselves to find answers to the questions haunting us, the questions that keep us up at night and that trap us in the stuck places of our lives. We seek, we yearn, we ache for something more. Sometimes it even feels like we find bits of peace and fulfillment. But these don't often last, and off we wander, looking for what's next.

We've touched on this several times throughout the book, and I'd wager that every one of us knows what this feels like. The question I now pose to us all is, *Do you know how to go within?*

You see, we are used to seeking *out there*: making plans, picking a goal and pursuing it. Whether we came from religious or nonreligious backgrounds, we tend to get this same training. *Follow your dreams*, we grow up hearing, and we think that means we should have a picture of the life we want and then work like crazy to make it happen. Or we grow up hearing there is One Right Way to live, through the lens of our family's specific tradition or values.

"Follow your dreams" and "obey the will of god" may
seem like different messages, but they are actually
teaching us the same way of living: a way that keeps
us focused "out there" and out of touch with the god
within—and unprepared to welcome unexpected change.

In the "out there" way, we set our hearts on some outcome, some destination we think will make us good, happy, fulfilled, worthy, right, loved, safe, accepted—and we spend all our energy working toward it, longing for it, chasing it, trying to bring it to pass. We look to others to tell us how and who to be, and we lose touch with our own compass. The visions and goals we have of this might look different. For one person, maybe the destination is becoming a wealthy, respected, highly successful professional in society. For another, maybe it's living a life beyond moral reproach, becoming a figure of spiritual authority trusted by many and seen as a force for good in the world. For someone else, perhaps the vision is finding true love, meeting their destined soulmate and living out a grand romance together. No matter the dream, the goal, the outcome we have in our minds, the energy is the same: we are all focused *out there*, striving and longing to arrive in the vision at last: to get somewhere and attain something seemingly outside of us.

This is what it is like to live misaligned and miserable—to live out of sync with the god within. Instead, we must learn a challenging and unfamiliar, yet transformative, new way: to go *within*.

What does it even mean to go within? To go *where*, exactly? Is going within the same as the god within? Many of us struggle to know how or where to even begin to go within. Everything around us mostly teaches us to focus *out there*. What can we do in the world? Who can we become? What does god, Allah, Jesus, the divine essence, the Spirit, or the goddess want for me, and know is best for me? What things can I achieve in order to demonstrate my value to this world? But the trick is learning to remember that who you are, within, is enough.

> The reason you have value is that you are—not that you achieved this or succeeded in that, or that you are respected or admired, or that you have kids, a spouse, an amazing job, a fancy house or car. And by the same token, you don't lack value if you lack those things, even though society's messages would tell you otherwise.

We seek so desperately for our purpose. But we always envision that purpose as something we are seeking to *do,* not a purpose that we *are*. This is where *going within* begins. With an open heart and deep intention to seek out who we are, we begin to allow ourselves to just *be* and not only focus on what to *do*.

In the sacred book of my upbringing, many passages teach how to live in the *out there* way, the way focused on outcomes and visions, not aligned with the god within. My community eagerly taught these prescriptions: Here is the One Right Way that the god of the universe wants you to live, and your job is to work to fit your life into that predetermined vision. Whatever doesn't fit is wrong, bad, dangerous, and needs to be obediently sacrificed, or else your life will be ruined and you will go to hell.

I was very familiar with all of that. That way of living had nearly killed me.

Yet in that same sacred book, there is a surprising and seemingly confusing passage tucked deep inside that tells a different story. As I wrote this chapter, I had a conversation with my friend Kay, who reminded me of this odd verse. "Whether you turn to the right or to the left," it says, "your ears will hear a voice behind you saying, *This is the way; walk in it.*"

"How revolutionary," Kay said. "Instead of One Right Way, there are many ways to go. And somehow, it doesn't matter so much which way we turn. We could go right, or we could go left. Either way, our guidance will speak to us, giving us what we need." There could not be a better description of this profound shift from the "out there" to the *going within* way of living. It's not about choosing the right way, the right vision or goal. It's about our ears learning to hear that divine voice of the god within, guiding us in this very moment. And the voice does not tell us where our way ultimately leads. It doesn't always give grand visions to follow; it doesn't offer guaranteed outcomes. It just speaks quietly, peacefully, and warmly in our ear, helping us walk the path.

This is what it means to go within. We find our path not by pursuing predetermined outcomes and visions, but by paying attention to the ground at our very feet, and taking just the one next step that has unfolded for us, trusting the guidance of our god within to unfold the next one after that. We learn to have faith that we will be led where we need to go, even when it's clear that we don't know the next step ourselves, knowing our compass and the voice of the god within does: knowing that the love we need to survive will find us, and that we will be sustained—somehow—through the worst pain our lives will contain.

This way of living isn't for the faint of heart. I can tell you that much. But the way it will change your life is priceless.

•••

I wasn't always sure I'd want to *go within* again. After those years of leaving the church and losing my faith so spectacularly, I thought I was content hating god—flipping off cars with the fish bumper sticker, and getting downright angry if anyone even said the words *prayer, god,* or *Jesus.* But when I started to become friends with Dorris, something inside of me slightly opened. It was like cracking open a window on a cool fall day and allowing a slight breeze to blow through the screen. I still had the protective screen in front of me, but I was opening ever so slightly to possibility.

As she and I grew closer, I began more and more to allow myself to *go within.* Like a traveler in a foreign country, I was able to adventure and explore with her at my side much more than I would have been courageous enough to do if I were alone. In our conversations and exchanges, I began allowing my spiritual nature to show up in all new ways, to take some breaths of air, and perhaps most importantly, to *get curious*—which was in stark contrast to the way I was raised, which was to only follow what was already prescribed and laid out before me. This is what it looks like when we become seekers, wandering through the unknown and allowing ourselves to find what is actually out there.

The first steps happened in a way I never would have expected.

●●●

One day, Dorris sends me a recording of something she calls "an Abraham-Hicks session," which she says her friend attended. I've never heard that name before. "Who is this Abraham-Hicks person?" I ask.

"Well," Dorris says, no hesitation in her voice, "here's the thing: Abraham is an entity or group of beings that this woman Esther Hicks channels."

Oh boy. I have to slow down for a second. Talk about unknown territory...!

I have only a vague understanding of what channeling means. But I immediately recognize, somewhere in the back of my head, that if my mother heard this she'd say, "That is from the devil." And as her opinion whispers through the hollows of my mind, I hear myself loudly declare to Dorris, "Great! I can't wait to listen."

●●●

I know, right? I could hardly believe it myself. Honestly, for a moment, I felt stunned. Why was I reacting with such excitement to something so far outside my comfort zone? As a child, I entirely bought into my parents' ideas that astrology, tarot, witchcraft, magic, channeling, psychics, mediums, and all such things were satanic and evil. But now, all of a sudden, I was encountering the supposedly evil thing and having the opposite response. As I listened to the Abraham-Hicks recording, instead of feeling aversion, it was as if this light burst into life within me, and I said, "Where can I get more of these?"

I started listening to every Abraham-Hicks recording I could get my hands on—and reading their books, too. Then I started expanding out beyond that. I looked into astrology, tarot, energy healing, and more. And something inside me began to stir. I'm reminded of this quote by Albert Schweitzer: "In everyone's life, at some time, our inner fire goes out. It is then burst into flame by an encounter with another human being. We should all be thankful for those people who rekindle the inner spirit."

Dorris had certainly played that role for me, rekindling my inner spirit. She and I kept exploring, reading, listening, learning, and excitedly talking about it all. As we did, it finally occurred to me what I needed to be doing next in my spiritual journey, in order to keep rekindling that inner spirit: *Do the opposite.* More specifically, do the opposite of my parents. If my parents thought Christianity was the only way and that things like astrology, psychics, channelers, tarot cards, and everything in between were bad, then I was going to run toward that world and expand myself by learning about it. It felt so amazing to push outside of these norms and rules, the ones I had lived by long before I knew I could choose. Now, as an adult, I had grown strong enough to truly find my own way, to choose my own norms and paths. Though I was still struggling deeply with a lot of trauma, drama, chronic pain and illness, depression, and anxiety, I did at least have a sense of wonder and curiosity now brewing within me. And that was something I hadn't felt in quite some time.

•••

It's 2011, and for my birthday, Dorris has gifted me a reading with a woman who works with the Akashic records (an intuitive or psychic reading that draws from an energetic library cataloguing every experience, including all thoughts, actions, and emotions, throughout all of time and space). It's yet another thing I really have no idea about—but oh, man, am I all in.

In my reading, she tells me that I've always been in search of belonging, and in a way that goes far back beyond this lifetime to a pattern of wanting to remember that I'm not separate. "It was hard for you to choose to come into this life for this experience," she says. "The near-death experiences you've had were your way of knowing where the back door was—where the exits were, so to speak. They came to give you a glimpse and a reminder that there is more to this life than living as a separate human. But going forward, Alex, you will be able to do that through your meditation and other practices instead of through the near-death experiences." She also gives me specific information about family dynamics and patterns that there is just no way she could know about.

Then she tells me about a past life I lived as a witch. In that lifetime, my own family turned me in to the authorities, and I was burned at the stake. As she tells me all of this, something within me cries, *Yes! Yes!*, as though a part of me that has been forgotten is finally being seen, named, and brought out into the light. Even as I feel this, another part of my mind is making a connection: No wonder I've been behaving as though being left alone or abandoned is as bad as death. Somewhere deep within me, my very cells remember what it felt like to actually die alone as those who were supposed to love me left my side.

Because of these traumatic deaths, she says, I have a tear in one of my chakras (which I later learn are seven energy wheels or discs that run throughout the body, in a concept developed in India thousands of years ago; chakra means *wheel*). When I was burned as a witch, my second chakra, the sacral chakra, was torn. It's the sacral chakra whose primary function is pleasure and enjoyment of life.

That tear, she says, carried over into this life and then tore again when everything exploded with my family as I came out.

I feel it. As she speaks those words, they resonate within my soul, like something within me was literally torn apart. She recommends that I see a "shaman." Another new and unfamiliar term. I set it aside to return to on another day.

●●●

You might be asking, *Did you really just...easily believe the Akashic reading? Did you have any doubts about any of this?* Honestly, the best and truest answer is *no*, I didn't have doubts. I hesitate to say this, because I know these more esoteric parts of my spiritual journey might feel easier for you to digest if I said I had a healthy amount of skepticism about all this. If I told you that *I* was skeptical, maybe you would feel an important permission to be skeptical, too, because sometimes, with things that strain our credulity, we're able to stay in the room longer if we know we're not being forced to buy into something before we're ready—if we ever are. And that's really what matters to me the most: That we can stay in the room together. You don't have to take the path I took in order to go within. Yours may very well look different, and that's okay. Just be with whatever is true in you right now. If that's skepticism, great! It's all welcome here.

My own promise to you is that I will tell you the truth, and the truth at this moment in my story is that I was *not* skeptical. Writing this chapter, I pondered this deeply, looking at why that was. How could it be that I was so trusting of these things that might seem unbelievable to others? The answer, I think, was that I could *tell* this was my path. With the Akashic readings, the energy healers and shamans, I was—truly for the first time—following my own heart's compass, and the difference was unmistakable. Imagine that I had been taking a journey without using my navigation app, following poorly written directions to a destination that I hoped would turn out to be near my own. For the better part of the journey so far, I had been off the main road, stuck in detours, where the going was slow, confusing, and anything but smooth. I hadn't picked that route; it was selected for me by my upbringing. When I came out (or was outed), I definitely began to find a new course, but the going was still tough, because I wasn't in touch with my god within—with my own guidance system—so I was wandering aimlessly, trying to find my way.

In these moments when I dove deeply into my spiritual journey—into myself, truly going within—it was as though I had finally turned on my navigation app. Suddenly, the way was clear and the going was smooth. *You are on the fastest route.* If an accident or traffic got in the way, keeping me off the original highway I was meant to be traveling, my app rerouted me. That is what it was like inside of me as I began going within. There was just something in me, deep within my bones, that knew I could trust all the information I was receiving and that it was part of a grander plan for my life.

> **When you begin following your unique way, I cannot promise you what it will look like, and yours may not involve any of the modalities that mine did. All I can promise you is that you, too, will know the difference.**

One of the best indicators that you are connecting with that god within is that feeling, that "knowing" in your gut: THIS WAY. If you've experienced that in even small ways, you know what I'm talking about. If you haven't or aren't sure if you have felt it, stick with me; because my goal is to help you remember who you are.

•••

Now I was learning a new way of engaging with my spirituality: being curious, following what intrigued me and what felt right and true. The path before me was unfolding only a few steps at a time, and I honestly didn't know where it would take me. Often this unfolding happened in casual ways, or ways that seemed to come about by coincidence. About a month later, I was with Dorris and some of her bandmates, and someone was talking about their Akashic reading as well.

"There's a woman I know, Clare," someone said. "She's a healer and a psychic. She'll be in Berkeley visiting from the UK next month."

My ears perked up. "How do you get in touch with her?" I asked.

The woman gave me Clare's information, and I contacted her as soon as I knew she was in the States. We set up a session, and I drove to her, not having any idea what to expect—once again, no program, no guiding vision or set of rules to follow. I was practicing the way of *going within*, following this thread because something in it just *felt right*. It felt so foreign, so the opposite of what I had been raised to believe in, that I was able to open my heart and truly let in the energy of it all.

In my session with Clare, she immediately noted, "Intriguing. Your second chakra, the sacral chakra—there's a tear in it. I haven't seen something like this before." As I lay there astonished—I had only briefly mentioned the Akashic records reading and the suggestion to get energy healing—she began working on the tear through energy healing, using her hands, and what she could see with her mind's eye in my energy field.

I saw Clare several more times before she left to go back to the UK. One night, she invited me to a meditation group she was leading. She kept telling me that she felt something powerful inside of me, that I hadn't even scratched the surface yet of all the potential of my abilities. *My abilities?* I thought. *What could that mean?* At the very end of the night, she said to me, "I see you—I see you on this stage in front of hundreds of people. You're speaking, and it's a Hay House stage."

I laughed sheepishly, not sure what to do with that. By now I had heard of Hay House—they published many of the books I was devouring and sharing with Dorris—but I didn't have any personal connection to them, much less any experience giving lectures from stages.

To be clear, much of what I was discovering *did* feel confusing on some level; yet at the same time, I felt an understanding or an awareness that all of it was somehow true and really spot on. I wanted to keep going, to keep growing and learning. The fire in me that had almost surely fizzled out was starting to flicker and fan itself into flame again.

•••

In the readings I'd had by then, I'd received a lot of overlapping information from two people who didn't know each other—or, at the time of the readings, *me*. But both had said that I had spiritual gifts within me of clairvoyance, channeling, and powerful healing. I struggled to see how I could possibly believe that I had that sort of power and greatness, but even as I struggled, I knew I wanted to press on.

That whole year of 2012, I just kept going deeper. While my spiritual journey had begun to birth something new inside of me, in my outer life, I was also fast approaching the apocalypse time. So, as you already gleaned from that chapter, things weren't all coming up roses. After the apocalypse began, and once I got sober, I knew I needed way more help.

And boy, was I right.

•••

In those early days of sobriety, life didn't become easier;
it got harder for some time. This seems to be a common
experience for those of us walking the path of new sobriety
(of any type), and I think that's just because, when we remove
the substances we were using to mask the issues we weren't
willing or able to face, they all come rushing to the surface:
everything we didn't know how to acknowledge or deal with.

What surfaced for me was my own fear of being alone—of, as it
turns out, dying. In this area, my readings, memories of past lives,
and experiences in this life were all combining to show me just
how enormous my fear truly was. Meanwhile, the apocalypse was
forcing me to acknowledge that this fear was totally in control of
my life. I didn't know what to do about it, nor did I even understand
entirely how it had gotten this bad, but I knew I needed to face it
once and for all.

The first week of sobriety, I felt desperate, adrift, like my whole
body and spirit were one great cry of pain, calling out to the
universe, *I need help! I need some form of community—something—
ANYTHING—I need HELP!* I had long since sworn off church or
anything of the sort. But that night, something in me said, "I must
find someplace I can go, even if it's church." I felt crippled by fear
and pain, and I had run out of options. What next step could I take,
when I had no idea where I was going?

Taking a random book from my shelf and turning to its resources section, I found a website that let me search for local meetups. One result: a place in Alameda.

It was 10 minutes from my house. They had a service that next morning.

Sure, it looked like a church, but at this point—who the fuck cared?

•••

The woman who took the stage that morning, Ouida Joi, set something alight—a knowing, a sense that I knew her already. She felt so familiar to me. I spoke with her briefly after the service, and she invited me for a one-on-one session that week.

As I told her my story, she listened deeply. Then, when I'd finished, without hesitation, she said, "You need to see my friend Ruth. She's a shaman."

A shaman. Why was that word familiar?

Oh yes, I remember, I thought, startled. *My Akashic reading. She said, "You should see a shaman about that chakra tear."*

Here I was, back in the not-knowing: the way of *going in*, where I let the path unfold and just took one next step. I didn't even know what a shaman was entirely, but I took down her number and texted that afternoon.

Later that week, I walked down a lovely garden path and knocked on the door of a small blue studio. The door opened, and there stood Ruth, welcoming me with a heartwarming smile and a gentle hug. We sat down, and she asked for details about what had been going on, and so, just as I had done with Ouida Joi, I told her in a nutshell what had transpired: who I was, where I came from, and what I was facing.

There are many forms of shamanism, so I won't try to give a blanket statement as to what it is. I will simply speak to the work I did with Ruth and the training I received through her. Shamanism has roots across thousands of years of history throughout a multitude of cultures. Shamans have the capacity to walk between the worlds—both in the waking world, and in a meditative, altered state outside of space and time. They can often be seers and healers, and some cultures talk of those who could take on the pain and sickness of those they treated and transmute that energy. The shamanism Ruth practiced with me created times when, through drumming and a trancelike, meditative state, I was able to return to moments of my youth, accessing deeply rooted traumas, shame, and pain with the capability of creating healing and change that could ripple forward into my current self.

In that first session, I lay down on the couch and closed my eyes, and before I knew it, Ruth's soothing drumming began to transport me into some sort of meditative trance. Verbally, she guided me through some visualizations, and she helped me to meet, in this altered state, with some of my spirit guides—the first of which was a larger-than-life tiger.

This tiger was truly giant. His head towered over me and my six-foot frame, and he made me feel small—and not in a powerless way, but in a way that meant I knew he could hold all of me, which is something I haven't felt much of in this lifetime as Alex. He showed me that I could climb on his back and hold on, and he could carry me, displaying to me the vastness of his energy and power. His being symbolized willpower, courage, personal strength, passion, and conscious influence. He helped me see that he was always with me and had always been, almost like a guardian angel, even in the most challenging times of this lifetime. In all of the moments of my past when I was in need or in despair, he had been there beside me.

As he came to me in these shamanic journeys, I began to find ways, in the rest of my waking life, to lessen my anxiety and seek out my tiger spirit animal to help me in my times of discomfort and pain as I continued down the path of sobriety, trying to find a way forward in my life. I began to notice that many of my memories were gradually getting less charge and less pain around them. I began to feel lighter, less chained up to my past.

●●●

It's a spring afternoon in Ruth's studio. The tiger and I are going on a journey. Together, we travel to see 12-year-old Alex at the moment when he's sitting at the bottom of the stairs while upstairs, his mother tells the young man that he will burn in hell for being gay. The adult me sees myself—that young, impressionable child—sitting there, tears welling up in his eyes. I sit down on the steps beside him, and I put my arm around him. It feels like time is standing still. All the noise from 12-year-old Alex's house fades off into the distance.

As I take the boy in my arms, I tell him quietly, "I'm sorry—so, so sorry. You should not have had to hear that, and your mom should not have said those things to him." I tell him he is gentle and pure of heart. I tell him, "You're a lovable, beautiful child who is perfect just the way you are." Together, the tiger and I promise him that he is not alone, that we will be with him, always, along the coming years of his journey. I assure him that while it won't always be easy with his family, in the end, what will be best for him is taking care of himself and doing whatever he needs to do for *him*. I tell him that other people will always have their own ideas of what he should and shouldn't be and do, but that it won't be up to them—it will be up to him!

In that moment, I give my child self something no one else has ever given him: comfort and reassurance that it's okay to be just who he is.

●●●

At the time, I wondered, *Is this actually possible?* What an idea! Could I really use this spiritual practice to go back in time and tell myself all the things that I wished my parents and others could have told me? Could I actually have a completely new experience of being accepted and loved from the start?

The answer is yes. And so can you.

You too can journey to something from your past—
whether by journaling, or in meditation, or with the
help of a trained therapist, supportive friend, or, as
I did, with alternative healers—and tell the self of
that time the exact words you needed to hear.

We are all connected; we are oneness; and so, whether the reassurance and lovingkindness come from someone else or directly from you, it's all from the same healing source. Now, you might not have access to working directly with a shaman, or you may have no interest in that modality. (If you *do*, and you'd like to try a short shamanic journey yourself, you can download the "Transform Your Perspective" meditation that I have made available for readers of this book through the Hay House App or on my website www.alexreegan.com.) Ultimately, the method itself doesn't matter. What matters is your curiosity: your willingness to try out new things in your spiritual path, and to explore what you can tell is yours to explore.

You don't necessarily have to go as far out of your comfort
zone as I have. But if you remain only in what you have
always known, eventually those places will grow stagnant.
Instead, take one small step toward something new,
something that gives you that little flutter in your soul—and
let that lead you gradually into a new way of being.

•••

One day, a few sessions into our work together, Ruth asks me a question. "I notice that whenever we travel back to a younger version of yourself, you always refer to the child using *he* pronouns. Have you noticed that?"

Whoa. I pause. But as I ponder her question, I immediately realize she is right, even though I hadn't yet noticed it myself. In our sessions, we've gone as far back as the six-year-old me—the one standing in the driveway running through the sprinklers without a shirt on—and that little kid wants to be known as *he*. To go by *he*. Knows full well he is a *he*.

Holy shit.

●●●

As I continued this work with Ruth, I also worked with Ouida Joi. She was about to start a training course at the spiritual center: a prayer chaplaincy program. "I'm getting the intuitive hit that this would be good for you," she said.

I immediately recoiled at the word *prayer* and felt myself shrink back a bit into my fear. But then I considered: Ouida Joi had not been wrong yet. She had helped me through those initial weeks of sobriety and also directed me to working with Ruth, which had been exactly what I needed. Now wasn't the time to stop trusting her instinct. I had clearly been divinely guided to her doorstep.

So I stepped inside further, and I took her eight-week training.

> **It began to soften my heart and help me tear down more of the walls I had put up to protect myself. The good this did me was immense, because in truth, those walls weren't protecting me anymore—they were harming me.**

It was time to be a new version of myself in the world, letting go of the things that were no longer serving me, seeing them as tools that had outlived their use. I didn't have to hold on to this rage and anger at the church and god and everyone anymore.

I was ready.

You are likely ready, too, or you wouldn't be here right now reading this book. My hope is that this encourages you to look at the experiences in your life that are no longer serving you, to look at the tools that you might need to put down, and to allow for something new to come in their absence.

•••

Later that year, Anya and I moved to Austin. After some time there, I finally reached out to Ruth and asked her, "Can you train me to do this with others?"

"Of course," she said.

We did training for some time, and then finally we wrapped up our work, and I ventured out into the world to start working with others myself. Life soon began to change again. As my time in Austin wound down and I moved to Flagstaff, things did open up in new ways.

•••

One summer afternoon, I am sitting comfortably in a giant bean bag chair in my backyard, sprawled out with crystals all around me in a circle, my eyes closed, listening to a drumming track, heading off into a journey. I journey to this library in the sky, which is a practice I learned in a shamanic class I took.

As I walk through the library, I ask to be shown the book that, for some time now, I've been receiving messages I will write. I don't know how it will happen any more than I know how I might end up being a speaker on a Hay House stage, or how I will end up allowing myself to transition and actually be the man I know myself to be. But I go with it, just as I am practicing doing with everything else, allowing myself to be open and curious and seeing what happens next. As I walk through the library, with my tiger by my side, I'm drawn to one wall. I look along the rows of the books until I see one whose spine isn't facing out—whose title I can't read. When I open it, I am instantly transported through the book and land in a large room full of people. It is packed full, and in the distance I can see a stage, and sets of screens with something written on them. I begin making my way through the crowd and finally get close enough to read one of the big screens. It simply says, "Rev. Alex Reegan." I keep walking closer, and then I see myself, up on the stage, speaking to the crowd.

Shortly after, the image begins to fade out. I open my eyes, rubbing them as if I have just woken up from a dream. *What in the holy hell did I just see? Was that the future? Rev. Alex Reegan? How? Why?*

•••

After that journey, so many questions careened through my mind. Me, a minister—a reverend? I mean, heck, I was still feeling pretty turned off by the word god, let alone the church. But I didn't close myself off; I just kept sitting with it.

A few weeks passed, and I still couldn't shake the image. I called Ouida Joi and told her about the journey. "Well, I'm not that surprised," she said. "Makes sense, really."

I snorted. "Yeah, but are there seminaries that would take me? You know of any places that would be open to a trans guy, let alone a guy who doesn't believe in a traditional version of god?"

"Have you ever heard of One Spirit?" she said calmly. "I would look them up."

I got off the phone and did so. Their diverse, welcoming program looked intriguing. It was the end of summer, so I thought, *What the heck—maybe I'll try to apply for the coming spring, or the fall after that.*

The day after I submitted my application, I got an email from admissions. They wanted to set up an interview on the following Tuesday. I agreed. I spent the weekend in awe. What was I doing? What was I *thinking?* Even as I felt the fear and uncertainty, I wanted to trust; I wanted to go with what I had seen in my journey, and to follow the guidance I was receiving. It had taken me years and years of work, but I was finally getting more in touch with my Jack Sparrow compass and was intent on following my heart's knowing. I didn't want to give up now. So I kept going.

Tuesday came, and I had the interview. At the end of the call, they said, "We would like to welcome you into the program."

"Great," I said, astonished. "When do I start? Next fall?"

"We have a few more spots starting this year," they said. "The first weekend of classes is this Saturday."

This was too coincidental for coincidence. It just so happened that Dorris and I already had flights booked to New Jersey to visit her parents. One Spirit's seminary was in New York City, a simple hour-long train ride from her folks' house. Now, the beauty of this seminary was that their program allowed for students to attend even if they lived outside of New York. In fact, we had students in my class from as far away as South Africa, New Zealand, and Australia. Even so, I still found the divine timing remarkable: I would be able to join in person for the opening weekend of the semester. What were the chances? I know this much: When events fall into place like that, the universe is conspiring to lay out a path for us. So, once more, I dove off the deep end and into the unknown—this time, through seminary.

This is what happens when we get into the flow of following our heart's compass. When we use our guidance to take each next small step, trusting that we are connected to a deeper knowing that can lead us on our way, that's when things begin to flow with these kinds of synchronicities.

> When things are not flowing, our lives feel complicated, and we feel like we have to force or push the things ahead of us. When we feel exhausted, discouraged, and angry from shoving and trying to make things work, that's when we need to stop,

pause, and allow our internal navigation app to reset
itself, putting us back on the "fastest route."

Now, I wasn't looking for seminary, but it sure found me. And sometimes that's exactly what we need: the thing that finds us, not the thing we sought out, hoping it would fill us up.

•••

Seminary was a beautiful and challenging experience. In December, we studied Christianity, and I was dreading it. I had a lot of deep resistance still present. I found myself wanting to close down and withdraw. But my dean encouraged me to stay with it—to stay open and simply look at the fact that I still had a lot (a *lot*) of judgment happening. What if I pushed beyond the fears and the presumptions and tried, with an open heart, to look at Christianity, and the story of this man Jesus, with new eyes, and without the baggage I had carried forward all these decades? What might arise?

I decided to try. I surrendered to the possibility that what I thought I knew, I didn't. As we entered December, I let myself bask in the place of I-don't-know. And it was in that first year of seminary that I began to be able to use the word *god* again. The anger and fear gradually melted away, like hard butter melts in contact with warm bread. I felt a new sense of peacefulness in a space that had once been filled with angst, fear, and discomfort. In those first softening attempts, I knew I could—with time—overcome the religious trauma I had suffered, and learn to live in relationship with the god within;

to no longer feel as though I was on the outside looking in, but to embody the wholeness of the divine.

I soon began preaching in spiritual centers. Here I was, a trans man who had felt for so long like he had to exist only on the margins of this world. *Belonging*—it felt like something I could have only if I bent and molded myself to fit into the spaces that set the terms for my acceptance. But the truth was, those spaces weren't the ones I needed. In my early decades, I hadn't found my spaces yet; now I was finding them—places where I didn't just belong and fit in, but was also welcomed, desired, looked to as someone with deep wisdom and spiritual gifts that were needed in this world. All the work of going within was finally paying off in the external experience of my life.

> I came to understand that the work I did to find myself—to be myself and love myself—was what allowed for the outside of my life to shift and change too. It could not have happened the other way.

No amount of chasing the outside stuff will ever get us there. This is the key. This journey looks so external, like it's about what we are doing out there in the world. But to get the most out of this going-within experience you must do just that: *go within*. You must be willing to let go of the ways other people have thought you should do it, and instead reach within your own knowing to find what your heart's compass says is right for you.

My second year of seminary was focused on learning to perform ceremonies, from weddings to baby blessings, funerals to Sunday services. For our thesis or closing project, we had to create an entire book of ceremonies. I saw in this yet another opportunity for healing, and I decided to create a funeral service for the young man who had died of AIDS—the person I so badly wished I could have rescued from my mother and the wrath of her god. I wrote him a service celebrating his life, who he was, without asking him to change or be someone else in order to be loved and saved. I imagined a group of his friends and family of choice sharing stories about him, and his partner giving a message as well. I gave a eulogy offering up what I assumed was the exact opposite of the actual funeral that he received from his family.

As I spoke words of love and honor over a life where fear and condemnation had reigned, something in me broke wide open with healing and deep forgiveness—partly, even, for myself. Forgiveness toward myself for buying into my family's fear, and for the ways I punished myself for years for not doing something to stop my mom in those moments that she attacked him. I had wanted to save him from that experience, but ultimately I wasn't able to do that. What I was able to do was finally save *myself* from it, and all the trauma that it caused me. I felt a weight the size of the world lifted off of me in those moments—a freedom that I honestly don't believe I had ever actually felt.

Ordination and graduation came and went, and with them my experience at seminary. I made friends there who will be lifelong family of choice to me, and most importantly, I found more deep healing. I finally felt like I could move beyond where I had been and make room for something new. The going within made room for what would come next: my restoration.

Going within didn't solve every issue of life. It didn't make things perfect or turn every experience that followed into nothing but roses. And it won't for you, either. Life doesn't tend to work that way. But going within *did* give me relief. It made space for something new to be born. It helped me find ways to cultivate contentment and to just allow myself to be me. Earlier, I had been locked in the never-ending struggle of trying everything I could think of—that is, everything except *actually* going within. Now I was no longer afraid to be by myself. I had begun enjoying my own company, feeling at peace when it was just me.

I was ready: ready to come into my own more fully. Ready for what my journey had next in store, holding on more loosely and stepping into each day with a full, healthy, growing faith. A faith not just restored, but made anew.

Dear beloved being of the light, this is what I want to tell you...

Some days are hard days, filled with fear and anxiety. We have covered many of those topics, but we also want to spend some time covering the uplifting days, because you will have those, too. You will have days when you are in alignment with and connection to your higher self and your highest vibration, and things will flow and feel magnificent. These are the days you remember glimpses of you as a being of light and energy connected to all the universe and all oneness. Relish these days, beloved. Be enlivened and uplifted by them, because these are more markers that the big you has left the little you: moments to stop and breathe in the connectedness and the feeling of remembering who you are...even if just for a few hours, or a day or two. These are spaces you can build from.

Everything is okay. It is. Not "will be," but *is*, presently. Have faith in that. Have faith in yourself. Have faith in the years you've built your life. Have faith in the presence of your guides, in your compass itself. Rest in faith. Finally, at last, give in and surrender to faith.

Trust your heart, feel your feelings, be gentle with yourself right where you are, and above all, try to nurture faith in something—something true to you and your journey. Whatever you can find to have faith in is fine; the object doesn't matter as much as that you find it. You are a true being of light. You come from and are connected to all beings. Honor that, hold on to that, remind yourself of that.

Perhaps you had faith somewhere along the way and lost it, or it felt like something was still missing, but now you have the opportunity to recall that faith, that childlike faith, and live in that space with the missing piece at last in its place. The missing piece, for you, is the replacing of fear with love—replacing a fear-based god with a love-based god; replacing a world of scarcity and cruelty with a world of abundance and meaning; replacing a life that feels as though everything and everyone is against you, with a universe conspiring always in your favor. What a gift that is. When fear gives way to love, we have arrived in the true essence of the divine. It's all about Love—nothing else.

Dear beloved writing prompt

Tune to the god within and ask: How can I get in touch with the fact that my life is okay—my life is, not will be, okay? How might I foster a deeper faith in the universe, in you, in my own compass?

Write down the answers: "Dear beloved...."

CHAPTER EIGHT

RESTORATION

*"Our whole spiritual transformation brings
us to the point where we realize that in
our own being, we are enough."*
—RAM DASS

This work, this journey home to ourselves, begins to create deep new space within us. Slowly, we gain access to a place of renewal, as if we have done a home renovation. The walls of our home once sheltered us, yes; that is why we built them. But now the time has come for us to knock down the walls that no longer give us shelter, but instead confine us. We are undertaking a reclamation of our true selves, restoring in us the deep connection to our heart's compass, which brings us back into realignment with our god within.

This work is never complete. It's not a one-time event that we do and never need to do again. This is a commitment to a new way of living. We have entered a constant becoming. If we embrace it, surrendering with a deep bow to the divine—not as our boss, or something that is outside of and separate from us, but as the true essence of our being—life will unfold in new, meaningful, and spectacular ways.

This unfolding takes place because we are more powerful than we ever imagined or gave ourselves credit for. We are masterpieces, and yet we have always downplayed ourselves, lowering our own and others' expectations. For many of us, "Don't be a show-off" was the message we heard. We are ever constructing this brilliant lie that we are less than: not as smart, not as good, not attractive enough, less than average intelligence. Downplay, downplay, downplay. We aren't good enough. We aren't lovable. Even those of us who have grown outwardly skilled at enlarging ourselves, seeming confident and on top of the world, are privately consumed by fear that we're just one wrong move away from being found out as what we really are: a piece of *something*, but it sure ain't a master.

But what if we up-played? (Is that a word? No? Oh, who the fuck cares...want to help me make it one?) As I transformed, I decided that I would begin the process of up-playing: upping my game and working to see myself as connected to my true essence, which is smart, powerful, likable, intelligent, and spiritual. I would let go of the need for specific people to sign off on my worthiness, success, brilliance, skills, or lovability. I am the only one that needs to sign off on myself.

And I hadn't. Instead, I had played it small. The short game, the same game. Going for par rather than the eagle. I stopped adventuring and taking risks—especially with my life, heart, and spirit. I became tight, confined, pained, closed-off, stuck, and defined by my suffering.

When I was deep in the smallness one day, I watched an episode of *Grey's Anatomy*, where we learn that the character Teddy had never been allowed even a pet gerbil when she was a child, because with love comes pain. Her parents didn't think it was worthwhile to get her a gerbil only for it to die and for her to feel the pain of that loss. Teddy's whole character arc became evident at that moment—the ways that she had loved people but also always sabotaged her relationships, ultimately leading to ruin, because she was afraid of the pain.

That episode stirred a memory deep in me. In 2019, my pug, James Dean, died. For 14 years of my adult life, I'd had this wonderful best buddy; after he died, I said, "Nope. Never again. I'll never get a new dog." And I meant it: No way. But as I thought about Teddy not even having been allowed to have a gerbil, I flashed back to my own childhood.

My house was like a zoo. I'm not exaggerating. We had bunnies, hamsters, dogs, cats, guinea pigs, turtles, crawdads, fish: you name it, we had it. And each and every one of them, obviously, passed on at some point. Once, a hamster somehow got out of its cage and disappeared from the top of the five-foot-tall upright piano, never to be seen again. Life happened, which included both aliveness and death. But as a child, I never once shrank from this constant ebb and flow—never held myself back and refused to play. When a fish died, I asked to get a new one. When a cat got run over by a car, you could find me cuddling up to the other animals still gracing our home with their love and presence, never withholding my love. I always, always kept reaching out for more love, to give it and receive it—to be a part of life. I wasn't afraid of the death of those creatures, for some reason—perhaps because I didn't know too much loss yet, and I wasn't afraid to reach for more connection. Born-a-Day-Early guy wanted as much love as he could get. That hunger meant I wasn't permanently destroyed as each pet I loved passed on. Some wise part of me knew: The joy, the pain, the life, the death, they all go together in this twisted-up, heart-wrenching, beautiful, magical way. On an intuitive, spiritual level, I knew this was all part of the play, the hiding and seeking: things that disappeared, returning, surprising—who knows what comes next?

But that's not who I was for most of my adult life. It was as though I lost that playful, innocent, eager courage. When love seemed to end, or people or animals died—or even simply when relationships ended because they had run their course; no one was at fault, the tool was just no longer a tool—I didn't often run out into the world seeking more love, more to give, more to receive. I just didn't.

Sure, I put on a good front. I tried to be kind, welcoming, openhearted, and loving to folks on the surface level. I'd do almost anything to help the people I considered to be my friends or family. But deep down, where it counted—where the truth lived? There, I was keeping everyone at arm's length. And that energy wasn't harmless. It showed up in my relationships. My desire to try and avoid the pain of living, and my fear of what might come from trusting, ultimately sabotaged many of them.

Remembering the child I had been, I asked myself: *What happened?* What happened to that little kid who was willing to throw himself right back into the next box turtle he found on his family farm, to love that turtle and share the time they had together fully and wholly, with vulnerability and gusto?

Trauma happened, I guess. When trauma comes, we get small. Shell-shocked. Scared.

Sometimes, it takes a minute—or a decade—to find our feet again. That's okay. We get to take that time.

From the stories I've shared here with you, you can probably see why I closed down. I tried to hide because I thought I could protect myself from more pain and loss. I kept my true circle of friends very small. And when things got too hard, oftentimes, I would leave before someone could leave me. (I'd even move across state lines to avoid the pain.)

Many people who have known me throughout my life would say that they've seen and experienced my vulnerability, my friendship, my love; and that's true, but from the inside, I can tell it's also been diluted—masked. Each relationship was me standing in a suit of armor trying to hug someone. Yes, we were hugging one another, but there was always something between us—something between me and loss.

I thought about my James Dean this morning; my declaration that I'll never get another dog, especially another pug. I've said to Dorris, "Thank god I didn't have children; the pain of it would have killed me." I thought of all the *never agains* that we say, the loves we shut ourselves off from, because we're afraid. How much life have we missed out on by not stepping into the arena? As Brené

Brown says, in the arena that is life, we're gonna get knocked down; we're gonna get hurt and feel pain. It's part of the journey.

I've had a handful of surrogate parents in my life. Three out of six of my favorites are now gone. Would I give up the time I had with Harry and Creta Gerhart, or the time I had with Dorris's father Tadao, to avoid the pain that their losses caused? I spent 14 years with that pug right by my side. He was my best friend; he helped me survive many of my darkest times of depression. I probably wouldn't be here if not for him. Would I trade that? Would I give up those 14 years to spare myself the pain I've felt since he died?

I know the answer to these questions. Of course I wouldn't.

What about life, then? Would I give it up to spare myself the pain? Can I be here in this place, with all of it—the pain, the joy, the heartache, the magic, the love, the loss—or can't I?

How do I answer that question?

How will *you* answer it?

●●●

As I emerged from transition, going within, transforming, my answer to that question began to change. I could see more and more clearly that I had spent a great part of the last 20 to 30 years in some odd half-life, a place between living and dying, between loving and hiding. The question then became, *How will I spend the years ahead? Where do I go from here?*

It had become painfully obvious that I had downplayed my soul for years. I had squandered the level of commitment my soul had to me, and avoided the true picture it kept showing me: myself, as the powerful seer that I am and was intended to be in this life. I had neglected *me* for far too long. Enough was enough.

So I began to ask, how can I up-play? What can I do to drastically shift this space? In the midst of this restoration, I heard my first answer: learn to sell myself long, rather than short. Sell my knowledge, like an auction piece, to the highest bidder. I am a priceless heirloom, something someone misplaced in a dusty attic and later found again, only to take it on Antiques Roadshow and realize that what they thought was nothing more than their grandma's junk was really a precious artifact of this generation's soul-time on Earth. Now is not the time to play small and go for the short game. Now is the place and time to shoot for eagle—to be bold, be magnificent, as my soul desires me to be. I don't have to keep waiting around for anyone or anything.

Neither do you.

You, too, are a priceless heirloom, and this is the time of your restoration.

●●●

At this point, I want to return us to the truth we've meditated on throughout this book: that we do not *arrive*. We simply learn to adapt and continue to better embrace and trust the journey. Even in restoration, this is true. All the parts of the human experience are here with us, and that means the whole spectrum, from pain to bliss. But as we do this, we are also remembering that we are already holy and whole.

You might find yourself still asking, *What do I do when the aching won't subside? How do I keep going when every night is the same as the night before?* The losses and pains, they keep pushing you, wearing you down like the winds and rains wear down the canyons. And if water and wind can so evidently wear down solid rock, how much more so do these thoughts, these struggles and stuck places, bear down on us, beating across our brow—slowly, yet violently, breaking us to dust? How can we embrace life when this is part of the deal? How do we surrender to it, and what does surrender really mean? Does it mean giving in? Does it mean giving up? And how do we attain it? Are we lost in a desert, wandering from mirage to mirage?

It sure has felt this way to me. We do the work; we ask the questions; we are curious, our hearts and minds open. Wandering this world, we look for the next bit of direction, the next message or guidance we may receive, searching for our Jack Sparrow compass. If we're honest, we are usually hoping and praying that this time, the next thing will be the "one"—*the* discovery that will shift things more completely. We want each next thing—each next milestone, job, self-help program, relationship, guru, or achievement—to help us remove the blocks in our way and step into our rightful, true power, holy and wholly, completely ready for what life holds and walking forward with an open heart.

When arrival like this doesn't happen, we get discouraged. I know I get discouraged. Some days, our old issues rear their ugly heads again. Our bodies hurt: another headache, more exhaustion, the same old back pain, or a new soreness somewhere you haven't felt it before. Fear, anxiety: *How will I pay this bill? Will anyone ever understand me? How long until I have peace? Who is going to love me no matter what?* The list goes on and never ends.

Sometimes, I want a break. I want to take a moment, step off the ride, and just breathe: no bills to pay; no anxiety over this or that on my to-do list; no taxes, medical expenses, or chronic pain; no insecurities or fear. Imagine stepping off the hamster wheel into some magical moment in space and time where even our fear is removed—where our breath comes easily, and the universe and all its energy support us upright, held like a baby in a cradle. No fear...how do we get to that place? How do we step outside this experience enough to become observers of it, enough to lessen the physical, mental, and emotional pain that rips through us all on a daily basis? How do we find this sense of renewal, of newness, of releasing the past and resting in the present? Surely then, at last, we could fully and with hope embrace the opportunity to just be one in oneness. True, deep restoration.

What's the trick? Who has the key?

I hate to say it, but *you* do. We each do.

> It's like this whole while, we have been standing outside
> our houses, saying to ourselves, *Damn, I forgot the keys.*
> *How will I get in?* We stand outside, waiting. Thinking.
> Pondering. *Do I call someone? Heck, who can I even call?*
> *Who will come? Who will save me from this experience?*

Yet the deepest, most powerful truth here is that
there is not an external key we must locate, recover,
create, or find outside of us that will let us back
into the home that we seek. The key is us.

It's like we've been looking for a key—a solid piece of metal, shaped to fit this lock precisely—to a lock that actually functions with facial recognition technology. It's here already. The key it's here. It's us.

This will likely take some time to sink in, and in fact, I'm sure some of you—even myself, as I wrote this—are bucking the current a little with this one. Our ego wants to protest, feels incredulous. *Uh... yeah, right...I'm the key?! How does that make sense? How could I come to my own rescue? When the stakes are this high, who would instill that kind of authority in me? Who would let me have that kind of knowing, experience, and power?*

Oh, the answer to that question is even better.

You do.

You see, the mistake we have all made along this way is believing that we are separate and isolated from some god up in the sky. We have imagined—we were taught to imagine, and perhaps have taught others to imagine—that god is some other being, that he's in charge, that we are less than, and that here in this mortal life we are being punished or have altogether been forgotten about—unless, of course, we meet all of this god's specific standards and rules. Oh, yes, the rules. We must remember to follow all these human- and ego-made rules that we claim god made.

But do not fret, dear beloved; we are designed to forget all this understanding about our true nature so that we can actually become more powerful in the remembering. Most of us don't want to be the creators of our reality. We balk at the idea of being the all-powerful mighty one that creates this world we live in, because if we are—then how do we explain all the terrible, horrific things that happen in this life?

Having an external god feels safer around this question. We can answer it by blaming this external god, saying that they forgot about their children, and that suffering exists because god is distant, uncaring, weak, or cruel. Or we can answer it by blaming the ones who are suffering, saying that they aren't worthy of god's grace because they are sinful, and so they deserve to be left out in the cold, abandoned and forgotten. Or we can blame human elements: social injustice is to blame, or the Muslims, or the Jews, or the radical religious nutjobs, or patriarchy, or gay people, or liberals, or conservatives—the list goes on forever.

But taking ownership? Taking responsibility? Now that's asking a lot. That's a scary place for most of us. And yet, it's the exact place that we must venture to and explore. In order to enact restoration, we must allow ourselves to examine and truly understand who we are and where we came from—but even more importantly, where we are headed and who we are becoming.

We are enough, because we aren't separate from god; we are as much a part of god as one speck of sand is part of the whole desert. That's the conclusion we must come to if we ever want to find any semblance of peace in this place. This is what we must see in order to open the door to come home to ourselves.

And we have always had the key.

•••

Shame and blame are a messy business. Most of us have been looking down on ourselves in some way, shape, or form for as long as we can remember—joining hands, in one way or another, with what has wounded us, and keeping ourselves captive and in suffering long after any external forces are there to do it for us. We live in shame and blame for so long—directing it inward, outward, and everywhere—and find ourselves unable to enter our own restoration. We do this in many areas: the physical, the emotional, the professional, you name it. For one person, this might happen in school: You were unable to maintain the high bar that your family members might have set for you, so you began to put yourself down as stupid or incompetent, ending up at *not good enough*. For another person, maybe this showed up in your love life (or lack thereof). You have been telling yourself "the one" is out there, but you're not partnered when all your peers seems to be, so you start to think there's something wrong or deficient about you. Whatever the shape it takes, we manage to end up living in shame and blame about some aspect of ourselves.

For years, I despised my physical self, feeling such shame—even disgust—over this body that made no sense to me. I had always struggled with my weight and the ups and downs of what it was like to be in a human body that doesn't always cooperate with you. We are inundated with images, movies, and advertisements of supposed "real beauty," so what happens when you never really see yourself represented in those images—or you see yourself represented in the images that are supposed to be ugly, laughable, or gross? How do you form a belief about what you should or shouldn't look like? How can you help but come up with a completely skewed self-image? When puberty hit and my body began to betray me, that little boy who had fit in with his topless brother and friends playing in the sun and sprinklers was now gone. My body changed, weight was distributed in new places, my boobs got out of hand.

From a place of restoration, now, I want to take us back to these experiences of self-disgust, shame, and blame. And in order to get to that point of restoration, we need to take one more step in this journey: We need to learn to become observers. What do we see if we look at this familiar shame and blame from a zoomed-out place of observation, rather than from the zoomed-in place we usually occupy?

To illustrate, imagine we are at an evening in the opera house. (I like to use opera as our metaphor here, because it seems so dramatic to me. I have no idea what they are saying, but it always seems *intense*—and that's how most of us are in our feelings about our life: dramatic, intense.) Now, if you're *in* the opera—if you're on the stage as an actor—you're right smack dab in the middle of the drama. You *are* the drama; you cannot stand separate from it, observe it, see the big picture. But if you walk off the stage, into the audience, you become an observer. You have a new perspective on what is actually happening onstage; you can see how the parts of the play interact with and affect one another.

We can do this same kind of observing with our own lives, separating ourselves (even for a moment) from our role inside of the drama and stepping back just far enough to get a wider lens. This helps us find some separation from the thoughts, "This is happening *to* me" or "I *am* the drama, that's all I am."

With that imagery in mind, let's return to the example of my body and my weight. By high school, I had gained some weight; my boobs were enormous. I remember getting a physical and the doctor telling me I was obese. Meanwhile, my brother—who was my height, but weighed more than me—was never told that. *Huh... so different rules apply once again,* I concluded.

In the early years of college, when I escaped from my home life, I lost a great deal of weight. As the opera observer in the audience, I can see that that makes sense: I had physically removed myself from a lot of the stressful situations that were my family—hiding my sexuality and gender, the fear of religious condemnation, and so on. After I was outed, though, one of the only things that comforted me, in the midst of depression and self-loathing, was food. My grandmothers and I had always shared a special bond with food. They used food as a love language, a way to show how much they cared, and I needed that energy. Antidepressants and other meds can also have effects on our bodies. So over the next few decades, I continued this process of losing weight and putting weight on, constantly having to hear doctors tell me that my chronic illness would be helped if I just lost weight (to which I'd respond, "I'm so tired that I can barely get out of bed some days and am completely overwhelmed by aches and pains, but your solution is that if I just took on a serious exercise routine, I'd be cured? *Thanks for nothing, doc.*").

"Solutions" like that seem to promise to bring us into our restoration. Everything in this human ego form tells us to look at things through that skewed lens: that by doing X, we can definitely get Y to happen. This, as it turns out, is absolute bullshit. If we don't look beneath the surface and uncover the roots of our pain, fear, and dis-ease, we will never find the space to heal and allow ourselves to be whole and healthy. Remember, we hold the key.

That is why there's always more work to be done, even in restoration. Just getting rid of the surface thing doesn't often leave us feeling at peace. When we remove it—we finally ace all the tests, or we marry "the one"—we might feel temporary relief and freedom. With my top surgery, I did feel a peacefulness, but it wasn't The End of dis-ease, because I simply found something else to judge on my body. As we discussed in the last chapter, the peace we are all ultimately looking for is knowing that we are good enough, that we are worthy, that we are connected, and that we are truly not separate from anything, let alone god.

So where did my going-inside take me? It took me here. I zoomed out from the internalized beliefs about how I'd been bad by gaining weight, how I'd done it wrong, not eaten right, not exercised enough—all the things society tells us. I stepped down off the opera stage, out of the drama of this cycle, and I sat down in the audience. Then I asked my guides, my inner voice, the god within: *Be with me in this space. Help give me new perspective. Show me what I am missing.* And this is what came through.

In my mind's eye, I was able to see myself during all the times when I was just starting to gain weight again: When I was 12, after the fateful night with my mom and the young man with AIDS. After college, when I had been outed. After struggling into sobriety and during the apocalypse times. *Bam.* As though these episodes were being projected onto multiple TV screens, I was able to see all these experiences in a single, connected chain.

My guides whispered, "What do you observe here?"

"These are all connected to deep losses and painful situations," I said slowly.

"Look deeper," they whispered.

I looked deeper. Not only did each instance connect to a loss, but further: *I had chosen to see those things as loss.* I interpreted each event as something being taken from me, as opposed to the lens we explored in earlier chapters: that things, people, relationships, and events are tools for us. Everything is a tool for our healing, and sometimes that tool no longer serves us. It's not good or bad; it is simply making room for a new tool to enter into our experience. Good, bad—who knows?

During all of those explosive events, my ego told me that they were losses in my life, and that I must have been bad or broken for those things to transpire. But in truth, none of these experiences were losses. They did create vacancies, but these were not bad vacancies; they were simply *space*, so that something entirely new could come in—so that I might actually birth something new. I couldn't have birthed my current life if these spaces had not come first. The 12-year-old's loss of innocence led me to realize that I was attracted to women. Ultimately, if not right then, knowing who we might find attraction and partnership with is a great gift. Being outed exploded my life, yes; but my life *needed* to be exploded, because it was already harming me—and that made me leave, venture out beyond where I had been and *who* I had been, ultimately finding healthier and more growthful places in the world outside of what I had known. I certainly would never have left if I hadn't been propelled like a rocket ship out of that former life. The time of the apocalypse, the sobriety, losing Creta, and just a few years later, Harry too—all of these events shot me inward, toward deeper healing work. They helped me clear out enough of the debris so that I could transition, become fully myself, change my life entirely, find Dorris again, and reclaim my spirituality by going within.

Entering restoration, I could see all these events from the zoomed-out position of the observer. And sure enough, the work continued. Only a few years after we lost Creta and Harry, my father-in-law passed away, suddenly and unexpectedly. I had had family with him and his wife: people who accepted and welcomed me, loved me for who I was. He hadn't questioned using my male pronouns, but had simply taken me as I was—in all my greatness, not in spite of my shortcomings.

Loss, right? Surely this was loss: pure and simple.

Yet my new framework was here to remind me to zoom out and get curious about what I might see if I looked from the position of the observer. Weeks after his passing, sitting in my wife's childhood bedroom, I was processing what had just happened and what we would all face next. In the throes of a winter that now seemed even harder, I sat down with my book manuscript; only months before, I had almost deleted the whole thing, thinking to myself, *Why bother? What could come of this?* Now, I sat there reading through what I had already written. I finished and closed the laptop, wiping tears from my eyes and genuinely feeling a sense of relief and peace, as I heard my still, small voice—and a hint of my father-in-law's voice, as well—say, *Finish this.* And so I did.

In telling the story, I could see what the observer saw. I could see the arcs of meaning and restoration taking shape. From the zoomed-in, limited perspective at any given point in my journey, all I could see and feel was the drama of the suffering. All of my life, I spent time judging myself for not doing things properly, not following how society or my family said I should be able to do it— whether that was my sexuality, my beliefs, my gender, my weight, my thoughts, or even the way I acted and was in the world. In restoration, a broader perspective arrived. I could see how, for everything that had transpired in my life, I had the opportunity to take it and make it a part of the beauty of what I birthed next.

The restoration in all this is about surrendering. As we move forward in our journey, we do so with a new posture of surrender—open to I-don't-know, curious and vulnerable, surrendering our ego's idea that it knows how life is supposed to go, and instead being willing to be taken to places we did not imagine. We become willing to look from the observer's perspective, not from our zoomed-in perspective as the actor on the stage, where we don't have a lot of clarity and can only see things one way.

This was my own most profound and lasting restoration. But using the technique of stepping into the audience and asking for the god within—for my guides, ancestors, angels, spirit animals, the oneness—to step into the space with me, to open up my eyes and shift my perspective anew, that is what began to change it all and restore my peace, to soothe my pain and restore my heart.

I had some actual restoration with people in my life as well, Dorris, of course, being the first and most impactful example. But there were others. I had been close with my cousin, the one whose parents outed me to my parents, for most of our early lives. In the aftermath of that situation, we ended up being estranged for many years. But the beauty of doing this internal healing work is that you never know how it will manifest in the external world as you heal. She and I found our way back to one another. She has kids now and a family of her own, and I am in their life. My brother has kids, too, and I am in their life; hopefully, with the presence of my story in their hearts, they will know that they can be whoever they are, love whomever they love, and still and always, they are enough and loved. That's just one generation after mine. In one generation, healing happened. That, to me, is a miracle and a sign of deep, true healing.

My parents and I have a relationship as well. It's not perfect; it's not something that is deep and vulnerable, which is certainly hard at times. And in some contexts, restoration is not dramatic or full, but small and oh-so-gradual. On a recent Christmas, while I was with Dorris's family and we were FaceTiming with my folks, my mom asked if she could meet Dorris's mom over video. I had been married to my first wife Anya for 15 years, and in all that time, my folks had never asked to meet her parents. Dorris and I had been together six years by this time, and my parents hadn't ever shown interest, but finally, that day, they did.

These are baby steps, for sure, but sometimes baby steps are enough. As I mentioned earlier, my parents still struggle calling me Alex and often use my birth name. They also struggle with calling me *he* and would never call me their son. But I've learned that this all says a lot more about their pain, their assumptions, and their own fears than it ever said about me. I don't have to take it on and assign its meaning as bad. I can choose to see it neutrally, from my zoomed-out seat in the audience of the opera. I have my own life to live, my own path to walk, and they will navigate theirs at the pace they need.

Healing isn't linear. Remember the image of the spiral staircase? On that staircase of our lives, we come back around to discover a shifted perspective. Time and space allow us to heal, and we see things differently—that is, if we choose to. This piece is crucial. We *must* choose it—daily, and in all areas of our lives. When we choose to zoom out and observe, we are able to take the lessons we have learned and the experiences we have suffered and transmute them into wisdom. We accept the I-don't-know, surrendering to the truth that though our ego thinks it knows how life should be, we simply don't. That is why control backfires while surrender births new life in us.

We learn to trust and hear the god within: not some god who is separate from us, but the higher power that we *are*. From this centered place, we do the internal work on ourselves, knowing that we can't get our family, society, coworkers, or anyone else to behave differently so that we feel better (and even if we could, that *feeling better* wouldn't last, either). We courageously and steadily go within, dropping deep underneath to the true nature of our pain and despair. As we do our own work in this way, checking our assumptions and the whys we assign, getting back in sync with our heart's compass and the voice of the god within, our courage and capacity grows. We become able to see what we *can* change about our lives, because though we were victimized, we are not victims. As we grow integrated and powerful, creating more and more healing for ourselves and others, we live in peace and union with our higher self, the guiding star of our heart's compass, which is leading us home. *Come home*, the voice beckons. *You are loved. You are enough. You are that priceless heirloom.*

We must choose to remember that we are not just these bodies, these names, these personalities, these identities or labels. We are *one*. There is literally no point where you begin and I end, because we are energy. And we were this energy long before we were all of the identities we hold now, the ones that separate us. Long before I was trans, or white, a Christian, an agnostic, a minister, or queer—I was before them, and I will be long after them, simply love. Just by reclaiming, remembering, and restoring this knowing, you are returning home. You are a grain of sand falling back down into the sands of the entire desert, never having been less than the whole.

So let yourself fall. And remember who you are.

Dear beloved, surrendering self, this is what I want to tell you...

I love you. That is what I want you to know. You are never alone in this experience—or in any experience. You are surrounded with love and light and the energy of all beings. Over time, you have been surrendering more and more, but sometimes it has been extremely difficult for you to do so. It is for most people. The ego trains you to think that you have things under control and that you're the best one in charge, but wow, is that ever a misnomer. Your perspective is so small; it's pinpointed. You need to shift your perspective to that of the eagle. It is time to surrender to your higher self and let that perspective take over; let it guide you on your path, as opposed to trying to continue to use your little field-mouse perspective to view the world and your situations, frantically planning ahead with the visions you want to create. In the end, all you create is suffering.

Surrendering to your higher self, and its understanding of the entirety of the universe and your experience, is what rescues you from your suffering. The bigger the picture, the better, and the more expansive your vision can truly be. If you are using a tiny field-mouse-sized lens, you can't get a very big view.

So today, be willing to let your perspective shift; broaden it—not by struggling effortfully to climb up on top of the house to see better, but just by surrendering to your higher self. Ask for help to see more clearly, more expansively, and to know that your true self knows where it's headed and what is best in each moment. You are held up; I am buoying you gently in these waters, and you can let go and float. No need to flail about. Relax, allow, and enjoy the ride. All is well.

Dear Beloved writing prompt

Ask the god within, your inner wisdom, the key inside of you, to give you guidance: What messages do you have for me about surrendering? Where in my life am I stuck in the perspective of the field mouse, and what will help me learn to shift to the perspective of the eagle?

Write the answers, beginning, "Dear beloved...."

WHAT NEEDS TO BE SAID ABOUT THE EMERGENCE

"Every problem emerges from the false belief that we are separate from one another, and every answer emerges from the realization that we are not."
—MARIANNE WILLIAMSON

Emergence—arrival, springing up, surfacing, advent, inception, dawn, birth, rise, blossoming, blooming, materializing, emanation—here we are. We have come to the final practice of this journey, and our time together will soon draw to an end. But not before we finish these last bits of work, hand in hand.

I told you in Part II: The Struggle that I wouldn't lead you directly to the answer because we were still *in* the struggle, but now we are here. Now is the time to share with you what I've come to know, truly and deeply, in my heart and soul. Now I will share what the Origin, the Struggle, and the Emergence itself have led me to.

We spent a lot of time talking about blame and the ego in this book. I also spent a lot of time in my everyday life talking about those same things. I spent decades blaming everyone around me for all the pain and heartache I had suffered. I was angry and bitter, high and checked out, disconnected and vile, afraid and alone. But I was also none of those things—I was also made of every bit of love, compassion, empathy, wonder, wisdom, beauty, grace, peace, and hope. None of us is ever just one thing. We don't exist in a narrow vacuum with a singular focus. We are a multitude. We are, in actuality, oneness. We are connected to all that is, to everything—to being.

What brought me to my knees was my need to finally do something different. Maybe it's a spiritual version of rock bottom: in the same way that eventually I hit rock bottom with my addiction to weed, I also hit rock bottom in my addiction to the blame and suffering that I was living in. I'd played those notes out until they had nothing left for me. The time came to leave blame behind.

What needs to be said—and what none of us want to hear, in our suffering—is this:

Right now, *you are at your own mercy.*

There comes a time when our inner work leads us out of the story of being at "their" mercy, whoever "they" are and have been in our lives: the parent who abused us, the church that lied to us, the lover who abandoned us, the friends who misunderstood us, the world that kept us down. Yes, there was a time when we really were at the mercy of those who hurt us. We make it through those times however we need to, and eventually we tell the story of what happened. It can be a precious time when we fully inhabit our anger story—until the day we realize that that story, too, has run its course. On that day, we realize: We are at our own mercy now. We must tell different stories. For new life to emerge, we must change our perspective and choose a new path. If we want true and lasting change, we must enter surrender.

That is what we are going to practice here, together. My hope is that this practice gives you the opportunity to learn new ways to zoom out and shift your perspective on events in your daily life, beginning to see how you might step forward in a new faith: faith that you *can* go beyond where you've been, faith that you can heal your wounds, faith that you, too, can emerge into newness, rising up out of your struggle, blossoming into beauty and love where your origin had planted pain.

This is the journey. This is the path back toward yourself — that journey home.

WHAT NEEDS TO BE SAID PRACTICE: THE OPERA

In the previous chapter I used the analogy of the opera. Our anger stories, which become our stuck places, are very much like an opera taking place on a stage. If you're in the opera—if you're on the stage as an actor—you're right smack dab in the middle of the drama itself. You are the drama; you cannot stand separate from it, observe it, see the big picture. You have no power; you can't stop what is happening. You feel helplessness. You have no agency. You're at the story's mercy. To survive, you feel like you just have to keep playing its game, read from the script you've been handed. That's what everyone else is doing, right?

When we're in the midst of a huge drama in our lives, or struggling with the aftermath of trauma, oftentimes all we know is rage. That rage feels like all we really have—it can even feel like the only real spark of us that is left; everything else, they took from us.

What happens, though, when we step off the stage? What happens when we gain a zoomed-out perspective and see things with a new eye?

To see how this works, let's take an example from a client of mine; we'll call them Jonah. Jonah was struggling with constantly feeling abandoned: by partners, parents, and so many other people in their life. In their current relationship, they were often set aside, neglected, and ultimately left feeling like they didn't matter, didn't belong, and weren't loved in the same way that their partner Caitlin seemed to demonstrate toward the other people in her life. Jonah was furious, hurt, and feeling vindicated in holding Caitlin accountable for her actions. So I asked Jonah to do this practice of the opera with me, and here's what transpired.

I asked Jonah to close their eyes and imagine themselves on that opera stage. "Describe the scene," I said. "What are the characters doing, saying, feeling?" Jonah closed their eyes and painted a picture of turmoil and angst:

> My girlfriend was sick, and I had just been sick as well. But I was recovering, so I thought I would step in and help her

recover and take care of her while sick. But she rejected that. It's happened again and again: when a crisis in her life arises, she tosses me to the sidelines, and I don't get to actually see her and spend time together. A month goes by, and we still haven't seen each other. Then, as she finds her feet again and goes back out into the world, she doesn't make a choice to hang out with me. She compartmentalizes me and doesn't prioritize me. She gives me excuse after excuse as to why she doesn't have time to hang out with me, but I can see her making time for everyone else in her life. The "off and on again" dynamic in our relationship is so intoxicating to me. It's almost like a drug of belonging. One minute she wants to be all in with me, and I'm her favorite thing in the world. Then suddenly, the rug gets pulled out from under me and she's seemingly all out again, and it's like I'm in withdrawal from the drug. I no longer matter, and I don't belong. When it's good, it's spectacular; it's like a roller coaster where we ride the ascent together. But at the peak, she gets off, and then the plummet down is always by myself.

"Okay," I said, "You've set the stage and described the drama you're in. Now I want you to imagine yourself stepping out of your actor self and looking back at it, almost as you would see yourself in a dream. You know that the person you are observing is you, but also in some ways not you. You step down off the stage, and sit in the audience, while your actor self goes on with the drama. I want you to look up at the stage from your new view. Observe the dynamics taking place, seeing the 'on again, off again' roller coaster from this perspective. Notice the you onstage loving the highs, being devastated at the withdrawals. Now, you are going to quiet yourself and ask for guidance—perhaps from your Higher Self, (think of your Higher Self as your big self, the part of you that has more access to wisdom and a broader perspective). Ask that Higher Self, 'What perspective shift can you show me about this drama on the stage? Does it feel familiar? Is there a pattern I am missing? What am I not seeing? How might I see this through a new lens?'"

Jonah sat quietly for a while, eyes closed. Then they responded:

I can feel how the players on the stage aren't our whole selves; they aren't who we really are. There's even a ridiculousness to the amount of drama I see on the stage. And I can tell this isn't the first time I've played this drama out. Caitlin didn't create it; I've been here before. My Higher Self remembers this dynamic. What's happening between Caitlin and me is just mirroring what happened in my childhood with my dad, who left me with an abandonment wound. From what I know of Caitlin's story, she has a wound like this, too. There is no one to blame or be at fault. We are both playing out our woundedness; it's not our essence.

From this perspective, I also have an overwhelming sense that I could just keep walking and walk right out of the theater, if I wanted to.

When I'm in the drama, it feels so real, as though there is nothing else—yet in truth there's a whole rest of the world beyond this one stage, this one drama.

We paused to take in this new perspective for a while. I could already see how Jonah's body language had grown calmer, looser, more settled. Finally, I asked Jonah if they were ready for one more shift. They nodded. "Now," I said, "You stand up from your seat in the audience and make your way all the way up into the balcony, far above both the stage and the rest of the audience. Now I want you to call in the divine, whichever word you use for that, and ask the question one last time: 'What perspective shift can you show me about this drama on the stage? What am I missing? How might I see this through a new lens?'"

Jonah responded:

> I can see the entire picture: the stage, the actors, the audience, the whole space. And we are not even our human forms; we are just love and connection, all here together. So, this thing that my 'self' feels separate from isn't true; I cannot be separate from what I am. Yet we're often removed from the "knowing" of that—that we can never actually be separate. Still, here in the balcony I can see it: The drama and the trauma are not who I am. The deeper truth is that I already am the thing that I am wanting.

As you notice, in each of these spaces, Jonah stepped back from the very zoomed-in perspective of, "This is me. This is my life. This is happening to me." Instead, they began to see alternative points of view. There was room to release some of the blame on Caitlin, the accused party—the one they had deemed the "perpetrator."

We all start out much more comfortable using blame against our "perpetrators"—but each of those people, just like us, are products of this world. They, too, are tired and confused survivors of the traumas that have happened to them, of the ancestral pain that has been passed down through their lineage.

We all carry within us more than we think we are carrying. We think that we are separate, isolated beings, and that what we do and what happens to us have no effect on the whole. But that's just not true. Everything has ripple effects that pass through our entire larger soul-body. In the exercise, taking those steps back made the external force of the issue smaller, as Jonah realized that their anger and the feelings they were having were a part of a long pattern that had been playing out many times in their life. Ultimately, they arrived at the deeper truth: They already are the thing that they were wanting. They are belonging. They are joined. They are oneness.

Now I want you to practice this for yourself. Come up with your own story for the opera stage. I know that in the past practices, I have let you select imaginary stories, or low-stakes stories, to practice on. But in this case, it's very important that you actually be vulnerable enough to pick a specific, real situation that's impacting you or a person from your own experience. This needs to be something that touches a nerve, something that pulls at your heartstrings—something that matters. When you write, I encourage you to be brutally honest; use cuss words if you need to. Get it out. Don't hold anything back in the example you write up.

At this point, I won't ask you to share what you write with anyone, but there may come a time when you are ready and willing to do so. And if you don't have anyone you trust in your life to share what you've written, you can send yours to me at an email address I've made especially for this purpose (operaglasses@proton.me), or by mail in care of Hay House Publishing. I would be honored to read it. So I hope you'll take a leap of faith, trust this process, and use your own story here.

1. Close your eyes and envision the situation as vividly as possible. Take a few minutes, if need be. Then write down what you see.

2. This time, as you close your eyes, allow yourself to stand up and move almost all the way to the back of the auditorium. Find a seat and sit. Take a moment to envision the scenario again; this time, observe the stage and the situation from this zoomed-out perspective. Ask your Higher Self, *What am I missing? What are my assumptions? Is there a pattern here? How might I see this situation through a new lens?* Write down your observations.

3. Now, envision yourself standing up and climbing a staircase to go up into the balcony, journeying to the farthest point away from the stage. Find a seat and sit down. As you take several minutes to reenvision the scenario from this new perspective, I now want you to call in whatever the divine is to you (the god within, Oneness, Creator of All, Goddess, God, Spirit, Jesus, Universe, Love, Life, Beloved, Father, Mother, Holy One). The word is not what matters; it

is the feeling and the essence we want to focus on. Now, take several minutes to meditate on this new perspective, asking the divine to open your eyes more fully and see what specific insights it has to share with you. Ask, *How might I see through the eyes of Love? What do I need to see to soften my heart and my discomfort or pain? What have I missed in my zoomed-in, 'small me' perspective?* Then write down the message.

4. Finally, I want you to envision yourself zooming out well beyond this theater, with such a broad perspective that you might see your whole life—not just the individual dramas within it, but the whole experience. Again, I want you to take several minutes to meditate on this new perspective. Next, invite the divine to open your eyes even more fully, asking, *How might I see my whole life through the lens of the god within? What would my life look like if I faced it daily from a place of union with the god within?* Write down your observations.

As I've asked you to do with all the practices, I hope you can take some time to notice what's coming up for you in your body and your heart as you look back over your responses to the scenario above. How did you feel beforehand, and upon completing it, what do you feel now? Do you feel relief, a sense of lightness? Less pressure? Less rage, angst, frustration, or aloneness? Do you feel more at peace, more in touch with your god within?

There is no right answer here. There never is. Remember? We never arrive. We just keep taking the next steps on our journey, continuing the never-ending journey home to ourselves—to oneness.

●●●

Here in the final pages of this book, we step into true surrender—because there isn't a "what to do next." In a way, that itself is the point; we are always so focused on the parts of us that must be doing, achieving, and checking off the next thing on our to-do list. But this is a moment of *being*.

Be-ing. I want to take that word apart for a moment. The suffix *-ing* means "one belonging to, of the kind of, one descended from." And *be* means "to exist or live, to take place, happen or occur; to occupy a place or a position." So *being* means to exist in or occupy a place of belonging—to be *descended from belonging*. Being isn't about something we do, something that we achieve or strive for. We spend so much of our lives feeling like strangers in a strange land, unable to find our people. We don't feel as though we belong—in our families, friend groups, at work—so we seek and seek with this ache in our hearts, all the while failing to recognize that the desire is to return to ourselves, to return home to oneness.

That process begins with unfurling ourselves from the chrysalis. We begin to take steps away from the ways we have always done things, to stop straying from our Jack Sparrow compass. We begin to choose the whys that are *not* worst-case scenarios just allowing us to feel vindicated in our blame. Think of how the caterpillar has that "small-me" sight, a very zoomed-in perspective—but when it transforms into a butterfly, it can fly, zoomed out, up to the balcony of the opera and beyond. At last, we can recognize that everything in our lives, our stories, our operatic dramas, is all a part of that one true pain: That we feel like we don't belong. We believe we exist outside of god—outside of belonging—outside of love.

Today, together, we come home to the truth. Just by being, we occupy a place of belonging.

We are descendants from sheer belonging—from the divine itself, not from Gods (with a capital G, signifying all the Gods we as humans have created that haven't actually connected us to the god within). We arise from the true essence of the god within, which is beyond words, and which exists only as a pure expression of energy and love. As we own this sense of being, we emerge as the changed, beautiful, divine butterflies that we are, able to soar to new heights and embrace our true essence.

This, my beloved, is everything. You, my beloved, are every thing: all that is. The I am that I am. Wholeness, oneness. Love. Surrender to that, and allow yourself to let go of the rest. This is where true peace lives. Your compass knows the way home, and the secret is:

You are already there.

Onwards and Upwards

"Begin to weave and the Divine
will provide the thread."
—Old German Proverb

To say that the end of the book signifies the end of my healing journey would be untrue, of course. As much as I have healed, my life continues to throw curveballs, new experiences, and, well, *life* at me—sometimes playfully, and sometimes mercilessly. The same will likely be true for you. But my hope is that our journey together in this book has given you a supportive framework to help you navigate difficult passages of your own path, and that the practices I've imparted to you will be ones that you come back to again and again, as I have.

I trust that you will find your way in your own journey home to yourself. If there is no place where you begin and I end—if there is no separation, and only oneness—then when one of us succeeds, when one of us overcomes, when one of us emerges from the depths of our struggle and the pains of our origins, we all do, on some soul level. So I will hold you in my heart, dear beloved. May the divine whisper in your ear, *You are safe, you are all right,* just as I once heard those words myself. You've got this.

Now off you go.

From the depths of my heart, I seek.
Light of the Divine, open our hearts.
Let my voice be heard.

From the hallowed halls of my mind, I wander.
Light of the Divine, open our hearts.
Let my thoughts be stilled.

From the veins of my ancestors, I pulse.
Light of the Divine, open our hearts.
Let my past be healed.

From the deepest yearning of the soul, I speak.
Light of the Divine, open our hearts.
Let my desires be heard.

We seek and wander, pulse and speak.
Light of the Divine, open our hearts.
May unconditional acceptance and love shine upon us.

—ALEX REEGAN AND DORRIS MURAMATSU

RECOMMENDED RESOURCES

Books

Walking Through Anger: A New Design for Confronting Conflict in an Emotionally Charged World, Christian Conte. (Sounds True, 2019)

Illogical: Saying Yes to Life Without Limits, Emmanuel Acho. (Flatiron Books: An Oprah Edition, 2022)

Rest is Resistance: A MANIFESTO, Tricia Hersey. (Little, Brown Spark, 2022)

Untamed, Glennon Doyle. (The Dial Press, 2020)

Midlife Is Not a Crisis: Using Astrology to Thrive in the Second Half of Life, Virginia Bell. (Weiser Books, 2017)

You Are Your Own: A Reckoning with the Religious Trauma of Evangelical Christianity, Jamie Lee Finch. (Jamie Lee Finch, 2019)

Soul on Earth: A Guide to Living and Loving Your Human Life, Ruth L. Schwartz. (Six Directions Press, 2012)

The Choice: Embrace the Possible, Edith Eva Eger. (Reprinted by Scriber, 2018)

Set Boundaries, Find Peace: A Guide to Reclaiming Yourself, Nedra Glover Tawwab. (TarcherPerigee, 2021)

Audio course

The Power of Vulnerability: Teachings of Authenticity, Connection, and Courage, Brené Brown. (Sounds True, 2012)

Podcast series

We Can Do Hard Things, Glennon Doyle. (Cadence13, 2021–)

Unlocking Us, Brené Brown. (Parcast, 2020–)

Acknowledgments

To begin, I must thank six-year-old Alex, a child confused by the differences between how he saw himself and how the world did. Thank you for being you. To 12-year-old Alex, who suffered through the trauma of knowing that if you chose yourself and being you, you would lose a lot—and almost certainly, at least in your mind and that of many of your family members and friends, be banished to hell—I am so sorry that you endured that and the pain it caused for many years after, but thank you for choosing you. For being brave enough to be yourself in a world that is constantly at war with anyone who is different and not following society's rules. I am who I am today because of the bravery, strength and truth that my younger selves stood in, at great cost to themselves.

Dorris Muramatsu, how could I sum up in words what our relationship(s!) has meant to me over all these years? You helped me evolve and explore myself and my relationship to the world and the divine in ways I could have never imagined. You push me to grow, always, and to go deeper. You helped me find love for myself and others when I was so closed off and afraid of being hurt again. You shone the light on me in such a profound way that you helped me find myself when I felt most lost and alone in the dark. I love you always and in all ways. My heart.

This book would not be this book without Kay ben-Avraham having come into my life. And for that I have to thank Steve Austin. I hardly knew him, but his giant heart was clearly what he led with in this world. And Kay, I owe our work together and our friendship to him. From the little I knew about your background, I was worried you might not want to work with me. I was so relieved when the opposite was so apparently true. A lot of my life I've felt like my words have been lost in translation. It's often felt like I am speaking a different language than those around me, that we just aren't getting one another. But when you took my rough draft in your hands, it was like someone finally got my words for real. I felt seen in a new way. Then you helped me carve away at my rough marble slab until we set the angel free. I knew it was in me the whole time; I just needed a little help setting it free. So thank you, my friend, my editor, my family. Onwards and upwards: Are you ready for the next book?

Nate Borofsky, I love you, CF2. You have been such an incredible friend to me all these years. So much of this book is built upon amazing conversations we have had, trying to talk through our triggers, our pain, our issues with life. You're probably the only person in my life that I've never been too much for. "You're just too darn loud" was never something you said; instead you called me the Marshall stack. You liked my 11. You never have needed me to be anything other than exactly who I am, and I am forever grateful for that. Thank you for all the laughter, support, kindness, friendship and love. You're a spectacular human.

From the bottom of my heart, I thank Kezia Bayard-White, Michelle Pilley, and everyone at Hay House for taking a chance on me. I have loved working with every single one of you and I am beyond grateful that you helped me bring this to life. It felt so in alignment, so meant to be, all along the way. Anna Schnur-Fishman, thank you for your incredible contribution. Your polishing of the manuscript brought forth the true luster of my book, and I'm so grateful that I got to work with you. Thank you to Louise Hay for all the amazing work that you did and the foundation you laid, and thank you to Hay House for continuing her brilliant, much-needed work. You're helping the world in such deep and profound ways, and that is priceless. I have so much gratitude.

To Alice Gerhart, thanks for being you. For stepping outside of that group clique dynamic and choosing love instead of fear or hatred. Thanks for being family to me for all these decades. I'm not sure there are actually words to tell you what you've meant to me. We have always just been freely ourselves with each other, coming and going throughout our lives, but the gone was never gone, and we both knew that. The gone was always just "until next time." That opening line of "Mystery" by the Indigo Girls was sort of always my mantra for you: "Each time you'd pull down the driveway I wasn't sure when I would see you again." Their music always made me think of you. I remember the night I heard Girlyman the first time, opening for the Indigo Girls, the night after the '04 election, when I called you from the audience and held the phone up and said, "Oh my god, listen to this." I've carried you with me in my heart in all my journeys. Thanks for always being out there somewhere. "We're standing at opposite poles, equal partners in a mystery."

Harry and Creta Gerhart, wherever you are, I know that you know the gift you gave to me. Thanks for the extra family right when I always needed it. I miss you both dearly.

Hatsuko and Tadao Muramatsu, thank you for welcoming me into your family, for all the laughter, good food, good company and love. Hatsuko, you are such a character; you make me laugh and I love spending time with you. You are an incredibly amazing person and have such a big heart. Thank you for being you and being a mom to me. I couldn't be more lucky. I miss you, Tadao, but we feel you with us every day.

To Girlyman: How is it that music created by someone else can so perfectly become a soundtrack to one's own life? And not just to one individual, but to the many, many lives that you touched? Hearing your music forever changed me. Becoming friends with you all also forever changed me, both in so many obvious ways and in so many subtler ones, too. Your music and friendship helped me both to forget who I thought I had to be, and to remember who I really am. Thank you from the bottom of my heart. May you all know how truly special not only your music is, but each of you are. I feel tremendously honored to have shared in the experience that was Girlyman. You will always be the best there ever was in my book. Love you all.

Janna Kenniston, thanks for still being here, after all these years, and all this time. We have had so many laughs, cries, and inside jokes. We have shared so many ups and downs, the love of our pugs, and our beloved Yankees. You have been like a sister to me and I'm so happy to still have you and your entire family in my life. I love you all; you're my family.

Candy and Dudley Bacon, thanks for being a set of surrogate parents and a strong support system in my life. You two are amazingly kind, funny and wonderful people. I'm so grateful that the universe brought us together and gave us you as family and friends. I love you always.

Rev. Dr. Ouida Joi Cooper-Rodriguez, thank you for the years of mentorship when I needed them desperately, for the guidance and the compassion you showed me. But also thank you for the friendship and the spiritual connection we have shared. It means the world to me. I wouldn't be here without you. Thank you.

Ruth Schwartz, thank you for the work we did together all those years ago. You changed the way I experience the world and myself. You helped shine a light right where it was needed most, so that I could see my true self. You broke my world wide open. I could never thank you enough.

Clare Cusack, thank you for all the spiritual moments we have shared over the years, from the porch in the North Bay with S, to Berkeley, to Zoom and beyond! You helped me dive beneath the surface time and again and keep seeking for my truest self. Thanks for reminding me that I knew how to see.

Rev. Dr. José Román, thank you for your friendship and for *seeing* me and my potential. I'm so grateful for you and look forward to creating many things with you in the future.

Rev. Barb Hetzel, thank you for reminding me to go deeper, to be more aware of my judgments, and for being such an important mentor and friend to me. I'm forever grateful.

Gina Rudolph, thank you for your steadfast friendship. I always know you're there and that's a rare thing in this world. Thank you! I love you.

Alaina Levine, you're a true gem. Thank you for your friendship, laughter, and deep kindness. Keep shining in this world; we need more of that.

Michelle Grua, thank you for being family to me. For taking me into your home and making me always feel welcome. For all the fun and laughter, GoT nights, and burritos and for letting me be your dedicated IT guy. I love you.

Melissa Abell, first and foremost, thank you for your friendship. Beyond that, thank you for all the wisdom and spiritual guidance you've shared. You've helped me expand beyond my own self toward a deeper sense of the grandness of it all, and I'm forever grateful.

Jen Crow, thank you for your friendship and a bit of tough love at times when I needed it. You're a model of a surefooted, confident, spiritually centered being in this world, and I appreciate all the time we've shared together.

Emily Scott Robinson, I'm glad we found each other in this world. Thanks for your friendship, your inspiring music, the spiritual intimacy we exchange, the space you provide for understanding and exploring what it means to create in this world, and most definitely the voice memos.

Anicca Binkley, you might not read this, but this book is real in part because of you. You believed in me, even when I sometimes didn't believe in myself. You read whatever I worked on and gave great and uplifting feedback. I just wanted you to know that I'll never forget that, and I'm so grateful for all that you brought to my life. I love you.

Cat Calhoun, thank you for giving me the room to experience sitting completely alone with myself, which was the most uncomfortable and alarmingly nerve-wracking skill that I didn't know I needed. You gave me the space to find a new tool I hadn't known was in me the whole time—my own silence.

Rev. Diane Berke and the entire One Spirit Seminary, thank you for creating a space that respects and honors a multitude of different paths and faiths that we all know lead to the same truth of oneness. Thank you for helping mold me into the minister that I am and for the way you helped me see the world and my fellow travelers in new and meaningful ways.

To all of my friends over the years—from TR, the few of you from high school, and college, my seminary friends, those of you in Seattle, Austin, California, Arizona, Colorado, Connecticut, New York, D.C., Illinois, Kansas, Mexico, Spain and beyond—you know who you are, and I'm so grateful for you all. Though we haven't always been able to stay super close, it has been wonderful whenever we have been in touch. So many of you have supported me so deeply in this endeavor of my book (and in LIFE), so thank you for that. Know that I hold you all in my heart and send love your way whenever I think of you.

A, you might not read this, and that's okay. But know that I wouldn't have made it without you. Thank you for being an anchor through the roughest seas. The tether of your love kept me afloat and helped me heal and remake myself. I'm forever grateful. Always.

To my family of origin: I know it's likely that none of you will read this, or will understand me even if you do. And I'm okay with that. I know now that I didn't come into this life to submit to the rules and ways of being of the family I was born into, but instead, to expand out beyond what any of us could imagine—to be free, to be just me. I know I was never easy; neither were you. But I love you all. Most importantly, I forgive you. I hope one day you can do the same.

ABOUT THE AUTHOR

Alex Reegan is an interfaith minister, speaker, and transformative spiritual coach who uses his intuitive wisdom to help guide people toward their own inner knowing. Born into an evangelical Christian family that prevented his true identity as a trans man from emerging, he spent years in depression, anxiety, and addiction, trying to break free of the oppressive beliefs that bound him. His journey at last led him to sobriety, shamanism, and then seminary, which helped him reclaim his faith and trust in the Divine. Through speaking engagements, workshops, one-on-one and group sessions with clients, Alex is profoundly dedicated to helping others speak their truth, release shame, and find oneness.

www.alexreegan.com

CONNECT WITH
HAY HOUSE
ONLINE

🌐 hayhouse.co.uk   **f** @hayhouse

📷 @hayhouseuk   🐦 @hayhouseuk

▶ @hayhouseuk   ♪ @hayhouseuk

Find out all about our latest books & card decks • Be the first
to know about exclusive discounts • Interact with our authors
in live broadcasts • Celebrate the cycle of the seasons with us
• Watch free videos from your favourite authors •
Connect with like-minded souls

'*The gateways to wisdom and knowledge
are always open.*'

Louise Hay